Forew

This year, the Young Writ
competition proudly presen
best poetic talent selected f ... of up-
and-coming writers nationwide.

Young Writers was established in 1991 to promote the reading and writing of poetry within schools and to the young of today. Our books nurture and inspire confidence in the ability of young writers and provide a snapshot of poems written in schools and at home by budding poets of the future.

The thought, effort, imagination and hard work put into each poem impressed us all and the task of selecting poems was a difficult but nevertheless enjoyable experience.

We hope you are as pleased as we are with the final selection and that you and your family continue to be entertained with *Away With Words Devon* for many years to come.

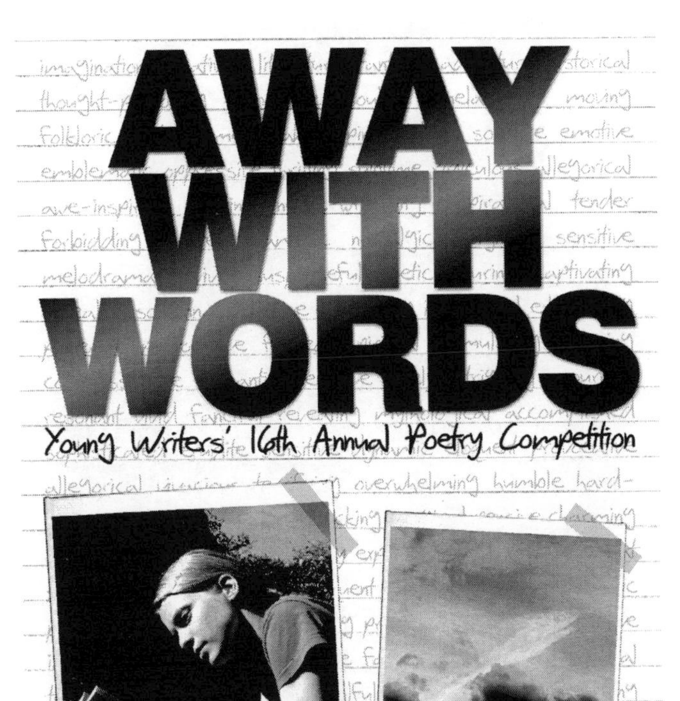

Devon

Edited by Michelle Afford

First published in Great Britain in 2007 by:
Young Writers
Remus House
Coltsfoot Drive
Peterborough
PE2 9JX
Telephone: 01733 890066
Website: www.youngwriters.co.uk

SB ISBN 978-1 84602 803 8

Contents

Stoodley Knowle School

Teignmouth Community College

The King's School

Trinity School

The Poems

Money, Money, Money!

Every life begins at birth,
Your lil' feet walk the earth,
People take advantage of life,
Showing no meaning to survive.

Everyone flees the country
Just to make a little money.
What is cash in this life?
Is that what we need to survive?

Is this what we need for peace here?
Flashing money to get somewhere.
Do you need to be rich to be someone?
Do you need to be rich to have fun?

Is this how the world is?
When it comes to money, who needs it?
So what, you're rich, you still will die,
Without money then will you wonder why

People laugh and people cry,
But still the world will end.

Amy Rusyn (13)
Bideford College

Why Were Friends Invented?

You have someone to watch your back,
Over to your house to make a pack.
Down in the dumps, they will cheer you up,
Then they will cover you in make-up.
They will ask a boy out for you
While you hide in the loo,
So that's why friends were invented.

Samantha Hall (13)
Bideford College

Dogs

He sleeps, he hides, he runs, he plays
Seven until ten without fail.
He's small but cute and sweet,
A cuddle I'll get, it is a treat.
He'll cry, he'll laugh, he'll bark really loud,
In my eyes he's just showing he's proud.
A pup is what he is,
But he will still never miss out on a kiss.

Friend and family this dog is,
He's one dog that can't be ignored.
He loves attention and his toys,
Nine weeks old and a silly boy.
He'll be loved and hugged until the day he dies,
He'll bring happiness and tears to our eyes.
What a great dog,
And that's no lie.

Chris Hill (14)
Bideford College

How Do You Know?

How do you know this is real?
That this isn't a joke and there's really such things as feelings?
How do you know that we aren't already 6-feet under
And a life is really for a lifetime?
How do you know that we aren't already famous,
That we aren't already on TV far in the future?
How do you know that we aren't living another's life,
And that they're living yours?
How do you know that this isn't a dream,
And that you won't wake up and live the same dream,
Over . . . and over . . . and over?
How do you know?

Emma Nailor (15)
Bideford College

The Meaning Of Life

The meaning of life nobody knows,
All we can do is just suppose.
Scientists believe in evolution,
But religion has a different solution.

The meaning of life for me
Is to be as happy as can be.
I want to work and I want to play
So I can enjoy every day.

I need to be warm and to be fed
And snuggle each night in my nice cosy bed.
I share my life with my family and friends
We like to keep up with the latest trends.

None of this really explains why we're here
Will we ever find out?
Perhaps one day it will all become clear
Or will there always be doubt?

Tamsin Ball (13)
Bideford College

Lover's Life

Life without you, I would die
because my life is perfect, you and I.
My soul would crumble,
over all the hurdles I would stumble.
Your eyes are all warm and glowing,
my love for you will always be showing.
In my memory, everlasting, is your smile,
to be with you I will cover every mile.

In my heart you will turn the key,
love and cherish me for all eternity,
for my life is dull without you,
for all my love shall be true.

Sarah Devon (13)
Bideford College

Verse

As
I
Write
I
Depend
Upon
The
Words
That
Have
Already
f
a
l
l
e
n
Fingers grip
with vowels on consonants
And head on paper. Younger years,
Unexpected words on words,
from fresh new mind.

Begin my journey as you read it,
grow before my eyes
with line upon line.
Uniform words on delicate lines.
Words from head
Verses from heart.
What loophole do I spin in?
What cycle do I spin in?
What circuit do I roam in?

Verses based on verses,
Rhyming based on rhymes.
Ink blots, smudges,
Jagged lines of burnt-out muses,
Neighbouring on white blank page . . .

Reluctant end . . .

Maire Beer (15)
Bideford College

The Word

Words have different meanings,
When uttered by different persons.
Though words weigh nothing,
They carry much weight.

But what are words?

A word is a word,
No more, no less.
A word just is . . . a word.

What do words mean?

Words mean nothing,
Words mean everything,
But nothing and everything,
Are after all,
Just words.

Why do we use words?

To declare unceasing war,
To declare undying love,
To forgive, to forget,
That is what, they are for.

Christopher Hyland (15)
Bideford College

Hattie

We've been friends for a very long time,
In fact, since we were born,
We started nursery and school together,
That's where we met Siobhan.
We made new friends along the way,
Erin, Katie and don't forget Kay.
Our friends are special,
Worth their weight in gold,
But Hattie and I will be friends till we're old.

Chloe Sweatland (13)
Bideford College

Different

To you I may be someone
Whose life is not worth a thing,
Where your opinions rise above the feelings
Which I may hold within.

Well tell me then, what are you?
Are we not both the same?
For I thought all of us were equal,
Not different in every way.

I know that our identity
Makes us all unique,
But we all have hearts inside us
And in unison they beat.

Our opinions they may be different,
Our looks may be opposite too,
But really you can't discriminate against others
Because they are not like you.

In my culture we respect each other
No matter what's been said,
In yours you fight over childish things
And some people come out of it dead.

I will not pass judgement on how you treat others,
As that is for God to do
And even though you may not believe in Him
He still will always bless you.

If I respect your culture,
It's common decency that you do the same,
For my identity may be me
But my culture is my way.

Laura Matthews (15)
Bideford College

Well, Well, Well, I Thought Punk Was Dead

Where have all the punks gone?

1970s, anarchy
Sex Pistols, The Damned and Blondie

Where have all the punks gone?

A day-glo Mohawk and ripped T
Oi! You look deeper, look at me

Where have all the punks gone?

They're not gone they're here
Punk's not dead, but that's not clear

Where have all the punks gone?

Now elite and underground
Demos and mix tapes circulating around

Where have all the punks gone?

Bands of today, rancid punks
Tiger Army, Psychobilly and GBH Skunks

Where have all the punks gone?

Here, Youth of Today
Not being drip fed by the mainstream pop they play

Where have all the punks gone?

In my eyes Minor Threat are still seeing red
As far as we're concerned, punk isn't dead.

Briony Bestwick (15)
Bideford College

Poem Of The Year

Icy pond to slip and slide,
Keep wrapped up warm or stay inside.
In the country, in the town,
Signs of spring are all around.
Spring has come, green buds swell,
Daffodils flowers in every dwell.
Sunny spell and showers of rain,
The cottage garden takes the strain.
Here's summer sun and dappled light,
Warm by day, still cold at night.
French beans run up their bamboo poles,
Strawberries swim in cream-brimmed bowls.
Sunflowers nod as bees buzz by,
Fluttering butterflies fill the sky.
Starfish, sea urchins in pools cool and green,
Shells for seashores you've never seen.
The colours mellow from green through to gold,
Some days will be hot, some days will be cold.
Trees feel the breeze with branches all bare,
Fireworks sparkle, fizz and flare.
The wind and the snow, the sleet and the rain,
Stay cosy inside by the fire again.
Under the tree you gently sift . . .
To find that special Christmas gift.

Zoë Floyd (11)
Bideford College

A Wish Tonight

Light, light burning so bright
In the stars I see tonight.
I wish I could last
Right through the night.
Sunlight burns so bright, so bright,
It shines tonight.

Sasha Floyde (13)
Bideford College

Deeply In Love

I loved you and I always will,
No matter what my love for you will always be true,
Till the end I never did pretend.

When you left me,
I cried day after day,
Hoping you would come back home to stay.
My heart broke into tiny pieces,
I was having a lifetime crisis.

I looked back on everything we used to do,
Every time I said I loved you,
I knew it was true.

Was it me?
Was it you?
To be honest, I don't have a clue,
All I knew . . .
It was over between me and you.

I wish we were still together
So you would be mine forever,
If only I could just turn back time
So you would still be mine.

Well I hope you're happy till this day,
Because all I can do now is hope and pray,
That you will come back to me some day.

Keila Brooks (13)
Bideford College

Orla

Orla is a crazy dog,
And sometimes snorts like a warthog.
She loves her mum -
You can't deny,
She growls at Dad -
Don't ask me why!

Kaye Martin (11)
Bideford College

Tears Of The Dragon

The nest had been hunted,
He was the only one left,
Those evil 'good knights'
Had slaughtered the rest.
He was one thousand years old,
His strength was beginning to ebb,
Spiders had started to cover him in webs.
The knights had killed them for sport,
They had killed them for glory,
So as you can see
How I must end this story.
He was sat alone,
A lone tear fell from his eye,
When the worst knight of all
Found his prize,
He killed him that day,
His heart was cold
And that's why there are
No more dragons in this world.

Richard Ham (13)
Bideford College

Poetry Day

P eople all over the world
O pen their books and read aloud
E very poem they like a lot
T hey even read the ones that are hot
R ich people read the ones
Y ou think are gone.

D ay is over for the year
A nother poem you will hear
Y ou have to read one another year.

Natasha Potter (11)
Bideford College

Frank Lampard

F rank Lampard, that's his name,
R ight mid is his game.
A mazing shot, he scored the goal! We won the game.
N ighty-night, we won again.
K icked the ball at the net, it was insane.

L ippy Rooney smacked in the face,
A mazing, was not a foul,
M any people say he is as good as a towel.
P layed 200 games the other day.
A mazing, it's a hat-trick.
R acing down the pitch,
D odging defenders to the goal.

Robbie James Murray (11)
Bideford College

One In A Million

Once shrapnel over my head,
Now concealed within the dead.
Soldiers drop like flies on a wall
And no one hears the colonel's call.
'Retreat! Retreat!' he calls once more,
But now a thousand upon the floor.
One mistake and die may many,
A soldier's cost is but a penny.
The end of the field is not but far,
But then I feel a mine ajar.
My foot is caught up in the wire,
In the distance I hear, 'Fire! Fire!'
Into the bunker, I shoot higher and higher
And that is the point my life does retire.

Ash Cory (14)
Bideford College

What If?

What if the world wasn't here?
What would happen to us?
Would there be such a thing as fear
Of anything anyone does?
What if we were never born
And everything just went black?
There was never a dusk or dawn,
Nothing ever came back?
What if the world wasn't here?
Not floating around in space.
No more smiles or tears.
No more human race.

Helen Smith (13)
Bideford College

My Wonderful Mum

My mum is the best mum ever,
She looks like a bloke called Trevor . . .
She's got a grey beard,
It looks really weird,
My wonderful mum, if you ever!

My mum is the best in town,
She always looks with a frown,
If ever you moan,
She'll turn you to stone!
My wonderful mum . . . the clown.

My mum's number 1 in my life!
She hates when I'm giving her strife,
But she'll always be there,
I really *do* care.
Run! She's coming at me with a knife.

Shannon Lamey (13)
Bideford College

Brightest Star

At first a sharp pain and then . . . nothing,
I could hear the cries of friends and family around me
But could not turn to reassure them that I knew what was happening,
I could only concentrate on from where I was laying,
What seemed to be the brightest star in the sky,
My little sister clung tightly to my left sleeve (as she did when
she was scared)
Weeping and at the same time calling my name over and over,
I somehow managed to whisper my last few sentences to my sister
Who paid much attention,
I told her that when I was gone I would be the brightest star in the sky
And would always be watching over her,
After that I could hear no more cries and then gradually see nothing.

Now I am just as I said, the brightest star in the sky,
And at night my little sister lies on the lawn staring right at me,
Crying and calling for me to come back,
But where I am now is a much better place
And I am a lot more happy,
Now that I am this beautiful star in the sky there are only
A few things that I do . . .
I sit here and watch over my family and friends as I said I would
And I wish that one day my little sister will move on,
Be happy and smile just like before.

Megan West (14)
Bideford College

Summertime

Summertime was fun!
We had a laugh in the sun.
We even went to Spain, all eight of us,
Traveling was tough but we didn't cause a fuss.
Summer '06 was really great,
I really am glad I have you all for my best mates.

Samantha Pow (13)
Bideford College

The Starving Earth

All around the world there is pain born of hunger,
There are empty mouths and despair,
As we watch from our luxuries aplenty,
Are we glad we're here and not there?

If we had food, because we had no choice,
If we were starving kids with no rejoice,
If we cried for help but we had no voice,
Would you hear this starving Earth?

If we had no rain and our crops wouldn't grow,
If a dust-filled land was the world we know,
Would you hold us close or let us go?
Would you hear this starving Earth?

Megan Downing (13)
Bideford College

Teachers

They're big and small,
Wide and tall.
They're male, female and maybe shemale,
They sit in a room all of lunch,
Away from the children who deserve a punch.
They shout and roar and shout some more,
'You naughty kid,'
And we are thinking, *don't pop your lid.*
But in the end they're here for a reason,
To teach and help us and keep us out of prison.

Alex Ely (13)
Bideford College

Friends Long Time

It's been a long time
But I still remember
The day you said
You would be there forever

When we became friends
We were in the first grade
You are one of the best
That I have ever made

I am here for you
As you have been for me
I am always here to listen
As long as you need me

I know sometimes
I am probably annoying
But that won't stop our friendship
It will always keep going

I know we have had our problems
But we are still friends
I know our friendship will last
Forever, until the end

If it rains, let it rain
The weather the better
They can't stop us now
We're stronger now, more than ever.

Andrew Spencer (14)
Bideford College

You Are The World

Robert Buckler, you are the best
You're like a present full of surprise
You're the driver of the world
The steam train giant
Your hair is like a field of rippling wheat
Dancing in the summer breeze
Your clothes project your possessed wealth
Your body toned to perfection
The intelligence of a child prodigy
You're the broom of all dust
The shovel of all dirt
Beside you every planet appears dark
As you rise higher than Everest
The power of a giant
Spinning the world's merry-go-round
You're the loins of all kings
Henry, Edward and Phillip
You are the guardian of all gods
Spying on the world
You have the angels of Heaven
Bowing down at your feet
You're a giant no storm can break
You're a man who men desire
Your style so slick, so smooth
Robert Buckler vos es orbis terrarium.

Robert Buckler (15)
Exeter School

Who Is Who?

Charlie Houlden, you are immortal,
You are supreme to all,
The messiah of today,
You are a god amongst mere men,
You defy,
You are the screwdriver that turns my bolts,
And the heavens open above you,
Neither Man nor God can deter you,
As you stride across mountains,
Your eyes are great sapphires,
In a great ocean of pebbles,
Your tears would cure illness,
But it's a shame that through your greatness,
You will never cry for as long as eternity,
You are the Alpha and Omega,
And show your anger in the form of peace,
You are greater than Chuck Norris,
You defy Steven Seagal,
You look down in pity to mere mortals,
The meaning of life lies in your deep mind,
But it is too great for other people to behold its majesty,
You are, Charlie Houlden, the greatest.

Charlie Houlden (14)
Exeter School

The Light Of Brezer

Brendan, you are a god,
You are a Challenger,
And a Mills.
You are a middle fifth,
You are the painting on the picture,
You are Devonshire,
You are the eyes of the world.
BMCM, you are the song of an angel,
The red on the rainbow
And the lion in the ring.
You are the pencil in the pencil case,
You are the stitches in a football,
You are the water in the sea
And the surfboard on the waves.
You are a genie from down under,
You are the pages in a book,
You are the lightning in the sky
That's clear and bright.
You shine through the night.
Your eyes are hazel and your hair like chocolate.
You are clever,
And you are like a feather,
Floating down to the sea.

Brendan Challenger Mills (14)
Exeter School

The Person Who Makes The World A Happy Place

Lily Davies, you are a goddess,
People bow at your feet,
And you rule the Heavens.
Your smile shines the world.
Lily Davies, you are a goddess,
The lake in the desert reflects you,
As your eyes sparkle with happiness.
The high mountains peaked with snow,
Shine with your beauty,
You are a river,
You are an angel.
Lily Davies, you are a goddess,
You make everyone smile,
And want to meet you and greet you.
You are kind and gentle,
You care, love and respect people,
You are our world,
Lily Davies, you are a goddess.
May you long live!

Lily Davies (14)
Exeter School

Self Pride

Jamie Rowe,
To me you are the king of all kings!
You are all that is to love,
You are the first, middle and last chapters of this book that is my life,
The shining diamond on God's golden crown,
The only *true* religion,
The single lone flower in the nettle patch in my garden,
You are the spice in my chicken madras, the cheese on my toast,
You are the joy in my life . . .
Let the whole world behold your perfection!
You have the climbing ability of Spider-Man and the strength
of the Hulk,
You can fly better than Superman himself!
You are my Alpha and my Omega, my beginning and end,
You are the cure for cancer, that is my sadness,
You perform the miracles of Jesus and you bear the wisdom
of Buddha,
No professor can beat your knowledge,
No orchestra can produce a sound sweeter than that of your
harmonious voice,
No one is more perfect than you!
Behold, the future and the present that is Jamie Rowe!

Jamie Rowe (15)
Exeter School

Who Is Who?

Katherine Bush, you are an angel
You are like a lamb to the world
Your power is greater than a giant
The stones will weep under your strength
Your eyes glitter like the rainbow's end
Your lips glow as pink as a rose
Your patience is calm like a river
And fiery like a waterfall
You are as brilliant as a diamond
You are an angel, Katherine Bush
You are the stone at the top of a mountain
The brick at the top of the tower
The river in every valley
The stem of every flower
With you around me, I am never lonely
Your elegance fills the room
Your smile fills my heart
You are as sweet as a strawberry
You are my everything and my always.

Katherine Bush (14)
Exeter School

Me

Richard Maddock, you are God,
You are perfect, a light in the mist,
The sun, the stars and the planets bow down to you,
You are the morning and evening, the day and night,
You command the elements, the Heavens,
The universe trembles at your anger,
There is no beginning without you,
There is no end with you,
Without you there would be no life,
The skies would darken, the animals would die,
You enlighten humankind,
The world is your oyster,
And you are life's pearl,
Richard Maddock, you are the meaning of life,
Richard Maddock, you are God.

Richard Maddock (14)
Exeter School

Ewan Harvey

Ewan Harvey, you are immortal
You are the loins of Allah
You are Mark, Luke *and* John
You are the winds of time
You are a man above men
You are the fire within the sun
You are perfect innocence
You carry a great burden
Which is also a great gift
You have hair of the purest mahogany
You're as strong as the Earth
As swift as the wind
As unpredictable as fire
And as fluid as water
You are the messiah, the prophet, the chosen one,
You are God.

Ewan Harvey (14)
Exeter School

Genius

Brittany Harris, you are a genius!
You are calm, you are fierce,
You are small, you are great,
You are sweet, you are sincere,
You are the essence of all life.
You are a genius, Brittany Harris!
With the voice of an angel,
You raise the heavens in which you reign,
The moon stays to see your shining face.
The waves rise to wash your feet.
You are Mary Magdalene, the saviour.
You are the prowling tiger, the diving hawk.
Your shadow casts light on places of darkness.
Your smile clears the name of marked men -
Who repent the sins of their hands.
You control the waves, you control the wind,
You alone can make dreams take flight.
You are the mountain rising from the sea.
You are the lake set in the desert.
Beside you every noise is silent.
Beside you every light is dark.
Every teardrop, every bloodshed,
Every plague, every illness,
Every cold, every heat,
Every drip, every flow,
Every cry, every whisper,
Stop. You are great.

Brittany Harris (14)
Exeter School

Who Is Who?

Connor Armitage-Lowe
You rule the world
You are the elite
The universe is at your feet
You are the Alpha and the Omega
The Father, Son and Holy Ghost
Do not even compare to you
The men change sex
When you walk in the room
All others stare in shock and awe
You are better than all the superheroes combined
You are the words in a book
The wings on a bird
A beam of sunshine
On a cloudy day
The world is in the palm of your hand
You are the coup de grace
Your looks can move mountains
Women die as soon as look at you.

Connor Armitage-Lowe (14)
Exeter School

Who Is Who?

Andrew Lines, you are invincible
You are the revelation
You are the Earth around which the universe revolves
You are the sword of doom
You are the apocalypse
You are the Alpha and Omega
You are the light of the Earth
All the world dims and bows in your presence
You are like God
You are the king
Behold his power
Behold him marching forth
The Earth trembles at your feet
Your eyes are like eternal pits
You are the cool breeze in the heat
You are the oasis in the desert
You are as unstoppable as an earthquake
Beside you every being seems weak
Every rock, every house, every tree, every bull
Every diamond, every cave, every earthquake, every gale.

Andrew Lines (14)
Exeter School

Who Is Who?

Jack Niven, you steer the train of life through
The tunnel of love across the world
You rise where others fall
You are the sweet nectar from a tropical plant.
You are the meaning of life
You are as soft as a pillow but as hard as steel
Tu est fantastique
You are the guardian of God
You are the eighth wonder of the world
Your eyes spread euphoria across the skies
God admires and worships you
Time slows down for you
Jack Niven, you are the world!

Jack Niven (14)
Exeter School

Wind Chime

W ildness, the rhythm of the wind blowing feelings everywhere.
I nteresting colours as the sun beams down and reflects lights
that you can't explain.
N othingness, you are sitting in a field of nothing - no wildlife,
no others, just you – the sound of a wind chime nearby.
D anger, strange sounds ahead - freaking you out of this world.

C haracter, the pictures you are looking at carved in the wood
and the song that enchants you and makes you sleepy.
H earing and awaiting the moments of silence in-between.
I mage, the dents in the metal or the burnt bits in the wood, the tones
of the sound are nothing you will hear the same or again.
M essages, running through your head, and then a rush of
thoughts take you away to a different land.
E ncircling, movements while the wind chime sighs in the wind.

Ashley Leanne O'Hara (12)
Exmouth Community College

Footsteps In The Dark

I hear sticks snapping around me
I hear birds squawking in the shadows of the trees
I hear bushes rattling in the corner of my ear
I hear footsteps all over
I hear voices whisper

I see trees shaking everywhere I face
I see lights flashing in the darkness
I see leaves falling
I see the sun being taken over by grey clouds
I see a bright green light in front of me

I walk towards it, wonder what it could be
I almost arrive at the attractive thing
I start to jog
I keep thinking, *what it could be - something or maybe someone?*

I start to sense a strange smell
I start moving around, suddenly it gets stronger and stronger
That's where the green light is
It takes over my attention
I go straight to it

I start feeling really strong winds. I fall over
I feel something touching me, turn to see - nothing
I feel a shiver in my bones, as if I'm about to be killed!

I jump back up and start walking quickly.

Billy Warren (11)
Exmouth Community College

Needle Fiend . . .

As the hollow pin of need draws deeper and deeper
the eyes grow wider and your will becomes weaker.
Twisted visions of darkening skies, hearing the piercing
screams of your subconscious lies.
Sell all that's to your name to earn enough for your fix mix,
as the demon in powder form starts working his mind tricks.
Waves of paranoia intercept, manipulate, the previous
well-being which has now reversed, a change of state.

Screaming and panicking, shattering your thoughts,
cause and effect from the crack you'd snort.
If you'll have a good trip, you cannot tell,
it takes over your mind like a death-trap spell.
You long for freedom from the pain and torture,
having clouded visions, just thoughts with no order.
Decaying smiles, and weeks without laughter,
a lack of control, you are no longer your master.
It started in your childhood as the attacks bled numb,
you see hallucinations of what you have become.

Sleeping in your filth within a panorama of pain,
there is no future now, no hope, impossible gain.
The slippery slope of gradual decline,
the black hole of fear in trepidation towards demise.

You spent your evenings with lighters and spoons,
your future's a monitor reading, your body is a tomb.
The straitjacket so tight it's stopping you scraping,
your craving has won, you're eternally hating.

Like a thousand stabbing knives in the hands of a possessed army,
it hits you without warning like a ghost train, brakes failing.
Down and out, blood in your mouth. Flat line, but free.

James Gould (15)
Exmouth Community College

Why Me?

When I wake up in the morning my whole body is in pain,
The other people in the world act as if this is just a game;

I haven't eaten for at least five days,
All the crops have dried up, even the maize;

I look after my sisters and brothers,
And my starving, sick mother;

I walk six miles to get water,
We have no animals to slaughter;

I'd love to be able to read and write,
But to carry on living I use all my might;

If only the richer countries would help us out,
As we have no food in this terrible drought;

Maybe some day we'll have food and drink,
And then our life won't be on the brink;

I always feel jealous of the other girls and boys,
That can go outside and play with toys;

I look after my mother and try to keep her alive,
As my wonderful father didn't survive;

I worry what would happen if I got ill,
For my brothers and sisters, time would stand still;

My friends from the village feel the same way,
We all hope things will be different some day;

And when at last I get the chance to lie in bed,
Thoughts of a better life fill my sleepy head.

Beth Pollard (12)
Exmouth Community College

The Fear Of Death

Snuffling round my pen,
Not a problem in the world.
Fear rises, as Death walks towards me,
But, who is he?

A *bang*, a *crash,*
And I'm squashed through a door into blackness,
I panic. Where am I?
It smells of sour hay . . . it smells of death.

I move, but my legs don't,
There's not enough air, there's not enough light.
I hear my blood rush round my head,
Fear washes over me.

The door's open,
I'm free again but not for long,
The man is there,
And he's got friends.

A hand is behind me, it pushes me forward,
Through another door,
This place is worse, this is death,
I've entered the house of the dead.

I smell the lost souls of before,
Soon it will be me,
I get shoved through the stinking house,
Into another room, the man is waiting.

His cold eyes stare into mine,
He comes close but shows no emotion,
An object is raised towards my head,
Shock, heat, fear, pain, death.

The cleverest animal of the farmyard is dead.

Grace Jacobs (11)
Exmouth Community College

Stormy Night

I lie under my covers,
Knowing something might happen,
But what? I think.
I feel it in the atmosphere.
It starts raining,
Heavier,
Heavier,
And heavier!
I hear a gush of wind getting
Louder,
Louder
And louder.
Lightning strikes through my window,
My room lights up!
The thunder sounds like a humungous blanket flapping
round and round.

I lie there in my room,
Not as scared,
It is just a storm.
I am safe here now!

Evie Bunce (12)
Exmouth Community College

Out The Window

Out of the window I've seen,
the grass is green.
Something gives me a fright,
it's black and white.
A bird flying by,
I think it's a magpie.
In the month of June,
the flowers bloom.
All the colours of the rainbow,
red, blue, pink and yellow.
How I love looking out the window.

Stephanie Cain (11)
Exmouth Community College

Homework

Homework O homework I hate you I say,
I'll do you tomorrow but not today.
Homework O homework I hate your stink,
I wish I could wash you in the sink.
I'd rather take a bath with a man-eating shark
Or wrestle a lion alone in the dark.
Homework O homework I hate you I say,
I'll do you tomorrow but not today.

Luke Jackson (11)
Exmouth Community College

The New Sweet Shop

The bell sounded on the new wooden door,
Lots of many new things to explore.
Shelves and shelves of glorious treats,
Much too much for anyone to eat.
I looked around me and what I saw,
Lollipops, laces and candyfloss galore.
Fat, slim, long or small,
Sugar delights for one and all.
Candy, butter, boiled and mint,
But don't forget Cadbury's Dairy Milk and luscious Lindt.
Milk gums, bonbons and chocolate delights,
Get eaten by children every night.
Fried eggs, frogs' legs, snakes and snails,
Chocolate chips, spanners and nails.
Army and navy, candy twists,
Some of the sweets on your shopping list.
Jars and jars are on display,
Different sweets to try every day.
Sweets by the pennies, boxes by the pounds,
You have to choose quickly before the closing bell sounds.
The shopkeeper slowly turns off all the lights,
It's his turn now to taste the delights.

Hannah Walsh (11)
Exmouth Community College

My Smallish, Tallish Green Friend

I have a friend, he's tallish, smallish and green,
He's wicked in every single way
And he likes eating runner beans.

I went out with my other friends and he tagged along,
I was supposed to be back at 7pm,
Our usual hangout is the pond.

I got home at 12am,
My mum was fuming mad,
But once again
I blamed it on my tallish, smallish green friend!

Ashley Newcombe (12)
Exmouth Community College

My Magic Box

(Based on 'Magic Box' by Kit Wright)

I will put in my box . . .
The first ever war,
The biggest wave of the Atlantic,
The Earth at one day old.

I will put in my box . . .
The atomic bomb hitting the floor,
The sea swishing under my feet,
The snow crunching under my feet.

I will put in my box . . .
The first ever smell of a kebab shop,
The smell of some candyfloss.

I will put in my box . . .
The best biker in the world,
The biggest ramp in the world
And the biggest pizza in the universe.

My box roof is a bike frame
And gold corners,
And never melting chocolate.

Greg Shambrook (12)
Great Torrington School

My Magic Box

(Based on 'Magic Box' by Kit Wright)

I will put in the box . . .
The highest mountains in Austria with mist surrounding the top,
The largest lakes in Switzerland with the clearest water ever,
Some of the great views and things I have ever seen,
A steam train going through the Scottish mountains,
A key to a mysterious castle.

I will put in the box . . .
My favourite music, pop stars and bands,
A group of birds singing in the countryside of Devon,
The first ever word my younger brother said.

I will put in the box . . .
A fresh meadow full of poppies,
The sweet smell of a rose,
The smell of melting chocolate in a chocolate factory.

I will put in the box . . .
A pinch of velvet from the midnight sky,
A touch of silk fresh from the plant.

I will put in the box . . .
The gush of wind on a pretty coastal path,
The happy smile from all my friends,
The breath of a summer sun.

I will put in the box . . .
A wish of having a money tree,
A dream of having chocolate rain.

My box is very special and it is made out of icicles and true silver,
It has sapphire stars and ruby rings and diamonds for the hinges.

This box of mine is kept in a secret corner in my bedroom
And not one person knows where it is.

Megan Hughes (12)
Great Torrington School

The Magic Box

(Based on 'Magic Box' by Kit Wright)

I will put in the box . . .
A cry of a newborn baby,
The sound of twelve sleigh bells,
The feel of crisp snow,
The smell of melting cheese.

I will put in the box . . .
The scent of purple lavender,
The laugh of my best friend,
The warm glow of the sun,
The feel of fluffy cotton wool.

I will put in the box . . .
The taste of warm baked beans,
The smell of freshly cut grass,
The sound of children shouting,
The sparkly glimmer of sequins.

I will put in the box . . .
A green sky and blue grass,
A day lasting only an hour,
A snake with legs,
A human without brains
And a day with no daylight.

My box shall be fashioned from . . .
Silk and rose petals
And the lid will be made of bats' wings.
My box shall be multicoloured,
With the stars and the moon and the sun.

I shall curl up in my box
And lie there forever,
And ever,
And ever,
And ever.

Elizabeth Allin (11)
Great Torrington School

My Magic Box

(Based on 'Magic Box' by Kit Wright)

I will put in my box . . .
A view from the Eiffel Tower,
A bluebird flying high in the sky
And a red rose.

I will put in my box . . .
The miaow of a kitten,
The first lullaby
And the laugh of a baby.

I will put in my box . . .
The net of a tutu,
The fur of a cat
And a fairy's wing.

I will put in my box . . .
Buttery mashed potato,
Melted chocolate
And a slice of cheese.

I will put in my box . . .
A calm, sunny day,
An amethyst jewel
And a rainbow.

My box will be different shades of purple
With golden corners, inside will be
The biggest stage to dance on with velvet curtains.

I will keep my box under my pillow
And keep it with me forever.

Emily Megson (11)
Great Torrington School

My Magic Box

(Based on 'Magic Box' by Kit Wright)

I will put in my box . . .
The twinkle of a star,
An enchanted island,
The roughness of rocks.

I will put in my box . . .
A baby's cry,
A flutter of a fairy,
A fork of lightning.

I will put in my box . . .
A secret world,
The sun from another planet,
The musk of my family.

I will put in my box . . .
A wizard on a pogostick,
The cool breeze of autumn
And the squawk of a crow.

My box is fashioned from aluminium and denim,
With icicles on the outside and food you can eat inside.
The hinges and lock is elephant's tusks.

I shall jump in my box whenever I want
And follow the route of the Internet.
I will put it in an ancient cupboard where all the dinosaurs live
And with all my family's magic boxes.

Sarah Ferguson (11)
Great Torrington School

My Magic Box

(Based on 'Magic Box' by Kit Wright)

I will put in my box . . .
The sparkle of a moonlit star,
An eclipse over Hawaii, like a black blanket,
A warlock on a galloping mare.

I will put in my box . . .
The twittering of the early birds,
The laughter of my friends,
That worthwhile gift of love that you'll send.

I will put in my box . . .
The silkiness of a filly's mane,
The feel of wind rushing at you,
The fun that always helps you.

I will put in my box . . .
A rainbow with a pot of gold,
A city that will never grow old,
A river of transparent water flowing gently backwards.

My box is of the finest wood, speckled with gold,
The lock, half a sword's handle from the bravest knight,
Right under your nose, the secrets are there,
But,
Only I can unlock *my* special box.

Libby Pullen (11)
Great Torrington School

My Magic Box

(Based on 'Magic Box' by Kit Wright)

I will put in my box . . .
Smooth, dark Belgian chocolate,
A lifetime of lollipops,
Three wishes whispered through long grass.

I will put in my box . . .
Jungle birds singing,
The scent of fresh-baked bread,
A ton of penny sweets.

I will put in my box . . .
A wheelbarrow of dark, passionate red roses,
A forest of money trees,
Warm misty curtains of rain.

I will put in my box . . .
My cat's beautiful miaows,
The shops of Paris,
The smell of fresh ground coffee.

My box is fashioned from platinum
With diamond stars twinkling all over it.
It's full of cherubs wielding bows and golden arrows.

I shall keep my box up in the clouds with angels protecting it
And my cat will be up there too, guarding the key.

Christina Hodgson (11)
Great Torrington School

Hello, Goodbye

'Hello, goodbye,'
I say in a nice polite fashion.
'Tuck that shirt in!' he will holler back.
His look of astonishment when the word 'No'
Travels out of my mouth and into his ear.
'Get them trainers off, this ain't no weekend school.'
'No.'
He burns up as people come to watch,
It's rush hour in the corridor,
Chavs, goths, hippies, punks, individuals, men, women, hobos,
Scum-to-be and some already,
Rubbing shoulders whilst trading insults,
Yes they *all* come to watch!
'Remove that hoodie!'
'Make me.'
People cheer and clap as round one ends.
'Get that hair up, belt off, and make-up gone!'
'No, no, no.'
'Do it or detention!'
His first real punch has been thrown,
'And spit that gum out! Wash out that pink hair dye
And everyone stop clapping and get to your lessons!'
It's their turn,
'No!'
They shout.
'Tuck in that shirt!'
'Can't.'
Get them trainers off.'
'Won't.'
'Get that hoodie off.'
'Cold.'
Get that hair up.'
'Short.'
Take that belt off.'
'Trousers.'
'Get that make-up off.'
'Ain't none.'
'Spit that gum out.'
'Chewing it.'
'Get that dye out.'

'Lovin' it.'
'And everyone stop clapping.'
'Can't.'
'Stop shouting.'
'Won't.'
I can't really say much
I'm in an after school detention.

Isobel Mitchell (12)
Great Torrington School

My Magic Box

(Based on 'Magic Box' by Kit Wright)

I will put in my box . . .
My ferret in her gorgeous cage,
My cousin Ellie and my family.

I will put in my box . . .
Fergie with rings of diamonds,
Rihanna, the girl of fame
And the Black Eyed Peas doing 'Monkey Business'.

I will put in my box . . .
The smell of a ferret just being washed,
A petal of a rose, the same smell of my mum,
The sound of raindrops gives me the sense of my dad,
The burning flame reminds me of my brother.

I will put in my box . . .
The fluff of my pet that flies high in the air,
A swift of hair that fills the air.

Burger and chips to remind me of McDonald's,
The chocolate that slides in your mouth,
Grapes that taste like raindrops.

My box is made with swirls all around it,
The colour is pink and in the corners are dancing fairies.
I will keep it under my bed which is a safe place.

Sophie Newton (12)
Great Torrington School

My Magic Box

(Based on 'Magic Box' by Kit Wright)

I will put in my box . . .
A picture of all of my family,
Sun Valley Holiday Park
And a Mazda RX8.

I will put in my box . . .
The sound of a running waterfall,
A cricket commentator's voice
And the mellow sound of clarinet music.

I will put in my box . . .
The smell of fresh air on a summer's morning,
The smell of hot melted chocolate.

I will put in my box . . .
The texture of king and corn snakes wrapping round your hand,
The feel of remote control buttons pushing underneath my fingers,
I will keep the feel of grass beneath my toes.

I will put in my box . . .
The taste of pasty and chips, spicy in my mouth,
The taste of celery with cheese and chive dip.

I will put in my box . . .
The colour green and the warm sun on the back of my neck,
The fallen snow on my cold hands.

I will put in my box . . .
The dream of being a PE teacher
And playing cricket with my idol, Andrew Flintoff.

I will put in my box . . .
A huge city made out of Lindt milk chocolate.

My box is made out of green oak and ash with red glitter
And the hinges are made out of koala bears' claws.

I will play cricket in my box at the best cricket ground
In the world – Lords.
I will keep my box hidden in a secret corner in my bedroom.

Paul Heard (11)
Great Torrington School

The Smugglers' Ballad

The sly smugglers schemed a cunning plan
They stole the loot then did nothing but ran
Some shiny silks, spices and brandy too
They schemed again with not much else to do

The ship was lured back to the yellow sand
The crew weren't best pleased to be back on land
The smugglers carefully planned and schemed
The smugglers sat as their faces beamed

The mouldering ship crashed against the rocks
The startled sailors fled in great flocks
Each lonesome sailor sorrowfully drowned
While every smuggler was safe and sound

None of the innocent sailors survived
Every sailor was forced to have died
Crying of sailors could be heard at sea
Each one of the sailors cried out, 'Not me!'

The gay smugglers arrived at the inn
They wished they hadn't committed their sin
Customs men waited for the time to arrest
They were taken away as they protest

The smugglers took their very last breath
Passing through the air was the smell of death
It's a long way down from the wood gallows
Shouldn't have drowned the men in the shallows.

Ellie Wonnacott (11)
Great Torrington School

Had Enough Of Love

Just the sound of his voice makes me tingle,
When I look into his eyes my heart flips,
He knows me and yet I remain single,
Longing for a kiss just to feel his lips.

His short brown hair softly touches my face,
His knee brushes mine unmistakably,
Just thinking of him I stare into space,
I can't even speak to him properly.

So, from a distance I stare lovingly,
Spending every day and night all alone,
He will soon love me willingly,
Wishing next year I won't be on my own.

There is nothing I would change about him,
But without his love my life is just dim.

Being in love with someone can be tough,
You may not even know which way to turn,
Even when you feel you've had enough,
It helps you in so many ways to learn.

Don't give up on love
And I won't give up on you!

Ellie Stacey (13)
Great Torrington School

Bored

I'm just so bored, I think I'll cry,
I feel I could curl up and die.
My friends have all gone out to play,
While I sit and waste my life away.
I'm thinking so hard it's hurting my brain,
But all I do is watch the rain!
I know it's there, inside my mind,
But the energy to do things I just can't find!
There are lots of activities to amuse me I'm sure,
But I've just never been this bored before!
I try and list all the things I could do,
But my thoughts are a barrier I can't get through.
'Boring people are bored,' they say,
But I'm just having a boring day!
I feel so blue, I'm just so sad,
And doing nothing's making me feel sad!
My brother's here having lots of fun,
And the jovial laughter's making me feel glum.
Everything is such a bore,
Even fun seems like a chore!
Does being bored have a cure?
I'll think of the happiness I could endure,
I can get through it, I can do it!
Maybe being bored . . . has nothing to it!

Genna Ash (12)
Great Torrington School

My Magic Box

(Based on 'Magic Box' by Kit Wright)

I will put in my box . . .
The sight of a tropical forest in Madagascar,
The sound of Spanish salsa music,
And the smell of my mum's perfume.

I will put in my box . . .
Fireworks in the Austrian Alps,
The sound of trickling water,
And the bustle of London Town.

I will put in my box . . .
Petrol on an evening bonfire,
The touch of my dog,
And cool water on my face.

I will put in my box . . .
The softness of snow,
A windy day,
And my mum's Sunday roast.

I will put in my box . . .
My family in later life,
Fish and chips,
And fire that does not burn.

My box is made of snakeskin,
Sugar and beads,
And the hinges are made from eagle talons.

I will drive in my box through South American cities,
And keep it under my bed for my last day.

Neil Thomas (11)
Great Torrington School

My Magic Box

(Based on 'Magic Box' by Kit Wright)

I would put in my box . . .
The sight of my pony on a summer's day,
All my pets' smiling faces when I come home,
My friends and family happier than ever.

I would put in my box . . .
The sound of gentle rain as it softly hits many rooftops,
People laughing at the funniest comedian around,
A million songs from around the world.

I would put in my box . . .
The feel of the silky, shiny coats of my pets,
All the fluffy wool
And a swish of silk.

I would put in my box . . .
The smell of slowly melting chocolate,
The earth when it has just rained
And the smell of the salty sea air.

My box is made from
Gold melted by the sun,
The rock from the moon as hinges
And stars for light.

I will put my box under my pillow,
My box will be invisible to anyone but me.

Molly Edwards (11)
Great Torrington School

My Magic Box

(Based on 'Magic Box' by Kit Wright)

I will put in my box . . .
The sparkly stars flowing in the midnight sky,
Five sweet kisses from a fairy,
The first giggle from a baby.

I will put in my box . . .
The taste of my own lemon drizzle cake,
A sight of crystal snowflakes drifting down on earth,
The sound of birds singing in the early morning.

I will put in my box . . .
A piece of soft white cotton wool,
The first step that I ever took,
And a hat that tells the truth.

My box is fashioned with turquoise blue buttons
And butterfly hinges with the calm summer sea
On the inside of my box.

I shall hide my box in a fairy's house
And I will keep the key always in my pocket by my side.

My special box!

Maddie Whalley (11)
Great Torrington School

Sounds Of The Sea

When the sea's in a rage, it roars and hisses and spits,
Throwing up spray as liquid diamonds,
Dark blue, green-grey reflecting the sky.
A wall of water, released and murderous,
Stay away from the sea in a storm,
Unless you want to die.

Zoe Thomas (11)
Great Torrington School

My Magic Box

(Based on 'Magic Box' by Kit Wright)

I will put in my box . . .
The wings of a falcon,
Diving down from the darkness,
The superb view of Giza
With the scorching sands.

I will put in my box . . .
The first touch of a baby
And the last sight of a grandad.

I will put in my box . . .
The sticky suck of a lollipop,
The mouth-watering sauce
That runs in your mouth.

My box is a crystal ice box
With a print of fire on it
And the hinges are made of platinum.

Bradley Hutchings (11)
Great Torrington School

A Friend Poem

F orgive each other's mistakes.
R espect each other.
I nvite each other round for no reason.
E veryone needs one.
N ever forget each other.
D on't give up on each other.
S ay good things about each other regularly.

Issie Haville (11)
Great Torrington School

There Goes I

The other day I had a thought,
About how lucky we may be.
Many people have harder lives,
Not like you or me.
They feel no love or support,
They don't get their own way.
But they don't shout or swear at us,
They don't know what to say.
What do you feel when you see all the homeless people
on the streets?
Is anything being said?
They have to live in a cardboard box,
Not a comfy bed.
When we are all cosy and snuggled,
All nice and warm,
They lay there numb with the cold,
Through the icy storm.
The tears fall silently,
They just want a hug.
The droplets frozen to their faces,
While we pass by looking smug.

She jumped and punched until her anger drained,
This girl is lost, she ran away.
Full of sadness and regret,
She has nowhere else to stay.
So next time you see someone,
With a tear-stained face,
Just look at them and smile,
It will fill them with hope and grace.

Tegan Sollis (13)
Great Torrington School

Charlie, Charlie

Charlie, Charlie, so evil and bad,
He walks in the door, mad, mad, mad,
With his pink belt
And blond hair,
Stinking of mud, killing the air.

He shouts to his friends,
'What's up dudes? How's it going?'
Teacher comes in,
Everyone's yellin',
Nobody even notices the teacher walk in.

Then Sam makes a paper aeroplane
And throws it in the air,
It suddenly goes quiet,
Everybody's still but one bad kid,
Charlie, is still moving, tipping chairs
And running round the room screaming,
'Wooh, yeah! Yeah! Yeah!'

Charlie, Charlie what a boy,
I don't think he's a boy,
More like a monster,
Eating everything in sight,
I wonder! I wonder!

Annie Keith (11)
Great Torrington School

My First Day At GTS

Excited and nervous,
My first day was here,
Early for school and full of fear.
The hall was so crowded with black and white,
Voices all over, it was a real good sight.

Miss Craig, my tutor, leading the way,
Down the corridors, silent we were,
As this was the start of a brand new day,
Settled and seated, the register was read,
And I now had to put on my thinking head.

Off to my first lesson,
Got lost on the way, oh and it's English I'm missing!
Cramming books in my bag,
Wondering which lessons I've actually had,
Break times are great, huddled in my group.
My bag is heavy, it is bell time again,
And I really should be ready.
It's my last lesson,
Hip hip hooray!
I've survived my first day!

Hannah Hutchings (12)
Great Torrington School

I Wish

I wish I could swim the Nile
Avoiding all the crocodiles.
I wish I could jump up high
And not have to fall and cry.
I wish I could be the best
And not feel bad about the rest.
I wish cake was really good
And not just an after tea pud!

Jonathan Johnson (11)
Great Torrington School

I Am Standing

I am standing on top of this skyscraper
I don't know what I am doing up here
Looking down on a tiny crowd
I feel like I can touch the sky
It just seems good to have the world seeing you
Looking at you
Wondering what you are going to do next
But it is you they are focused on
No one else but you

It is windy
I am shaking
I am cold
Shall I stay here forever?

Gaby Hagan (12)
Great Torrington School

Kymble

I saw it,
The vet was there
Putting him down,
It was near Christmas,
We were crying our eyes out.
Terribly sad, very sad,
I couldn't watch,
I needed to go with him,
I couldn't leave him.
Kymble was his name,
Kymble.

Kirsten Vincent (11)
Great Torrington School

Life

Life is a winding road,
Where you're deciding what route to take,
Wondering whether you've made the right choice,
Or whether you've made a mistake!

Life is a river,
Where you're just going with the flow,
You don't have any choice at all,
Of where you want to go!

Life is a roller coaster
You'll have your ups and downs,
But smile the majority of the time,
And don't have too many frowns!

Life is a load of random choices,
That you won't be able to take again,
But as long as you feel you've made the best of it,
Nobody can complain!

Daniel Lee (11)
Great Torrington School

School

School is cool
But sometimes boring
Corridors packed
People getting smacked
One at a time
Keep in line
Don't run
But have fun
Wear your woolly
But don't be a bully.

Bobby Plows (11)
Great Torrington School

Seasons

In the spring, the flowers begin to grow,
The grass grows long so we start to mow.
The birds do sing and build their nest,
The sun rises in the east and sets in the west.

In the summer, the days are long,
We put on a bikini with a sarong.
We sunbathe for a tan in the midday heat,
We pack up our car and make a retreat.

In the autumn, leaves fall from the trees,
People wrap up for the chilling breeze.
The waves get rough, the winds grow strong,
The days get short and the nights get long.

In the winter, it's all rain and snow,
The gale force winds are starting to blow.
We're planning for Christmas, there are presents to buy,
Santa's on his sleigh with reindeers that fly.

So that's the end of four seasons for another year,
It went out with a bang, a great new year cheer.

Kayleigh Newcombe (11)
Great Torrington School

Devon

D own one end of England, next to Cornwall,
E verywhere you look
V iews are magnificent.
O h, we are so lucky,
N owhere is quite like Devon.

Andrew Heywood (12)
Great Torrington School

Netball Crazy

All the girls like netball,
It's their new tradition,
Mini skirts, fancy tops,
The girls just love it.

Some like being shooter,
Some like being goalkeeper,
All the types of places
That you can be.

Yeah, someone has scored,
Ball back to the centre,
In the hoop once again,
Hip hip hooray!

Sometimes there's a rush of panic,
Like someone's just been killed,
Running around, it's a foul,
Dibbly, dabbly doo.

Hannah Pope (11)
Great Torrington School

Noises

There is a shouting in the corridors
Pens and pencils scratching on paper
There is laughing outside
Pages of books being turned
There is the buzzing of the computers
People outside waiting for PE
There are people coughing all the time
People whistling to cause havoc
Bell is ringing for the end of class.

Mark Tythcott (12)
Great Torrington School

Football!

Football, football is so great,
When they start to open the gate.
Fans pour into the ground,
To find their seats and hang around.
They are very excited and start to cheer,
Singing songs and drinking beer.

The players emerge from the tunnel focusing on the game ahead,
Fans go wild in anticipation, players ready to go head to head.
The referee blows his whistle, the game kicks off, no time to rest,
Each player works hard for the team so they can be the best.

90 minutes until the end,
I wonder who will score the goals.

Hooray, my team has won,
Liverpool has done it again!

Adam Davey (11)
Great Torrington School

Water

The water ran, the water flowed,
as it crept beneath my toes.
It swirled and whirled into the sea
and now it is above my knees.
It helps things live, it helps things grow,
it gives the world a greenish glow.
It gives fish homes and us something to drink,
it freshens the air and fills our sinks.
But we use too much, it's running away,
we use ten gallons every day.

Woody Reeves (11)
Great Torrington School

My Magic Box

(Based on 'Magic Box' by Kit Wright)

I will put in my box . . .
A griffin on top of the Andes,
A Chinese dragon turning the Earth purple,
The first sight of a blind man.

I will put in my box . . .
The roaring of a bear,
A CD of my favourite songs and tracks,
The chirping of a bird in the morning.

I will put in my box . . .
The smell of sizzling pizza,
The smell of newly polished furniture,
The smell of cotton candy at the fairground.

I will put in my box . . .
A slice of the finest pepperoni pizza,
A bowl full of ice cream,
A box of dark chocolate.

I will put in my box . . .
A person riding on a griffin's back,
A griffin jumping over hurdles and eating carrots,
A horse flying and eating mice.

I will put in my box . . .
The sun in my eyes,
The wind in my face
And the red and orange sunset.

My box has feathers for the cover,
An elephant tusk for a key.
I will take my box to the moon.

Ben Burgess-Dale (11)
Great Torrington School

Seasons

Summertime is coming round,
No crispy leaves are on the ground.
When you hear the cheeping sound,
You know summer is coming round.

Autumn time is coming round.
Crispy leaves scattered on the ground.
When you hear the crunching sound,
You know autumn time is coming round.

Wintertime is coming round,
Snow is piling on the ground.
When you hear the slushing sound,
You know winter is coming round.

Springtime is coming round,
Fresh green grass is on the ground.
When you hear the calming sound,
You know that spring is coming round.

And it all happens again!

Priya Singh Benning (11)
Great Torrington School

Friends!

My friends call me Lucy or sometimes Looby Loo,
They help me when I'm down, sad and blue.
I am always laughing but it's usually a giggle,
It makes my fingers tingle and my toes wiggle, wiggle.

I like red jelly and bananas too,
I look around with laughter, to see what I can do.
We do have our moments but we're usually OK,
We just get closer day by day.

Lucy Salmon (12)
Ilfracombe College

Blood And Ashes

Forever, I am falling
Flames lick my soul and destroy my heart
Or maybe I never had a heart? Who knows? Who cares?
This world of shadow and darkness is a part of me
And yet they tried to take it away
Oh, did you know that? Never mind. They paid.

Blood and ashes
That's all there is
Apart from the flames that ignite, flicker and die
I want to keep them going
Try to see this page I write
Oh yes, I'm on fire.

The darkness will never leave me
Like I will never leave this spiral
Round and round
All day, every day
Why would I want to leave?

Blood drips off the walls freely
Will I ever be free?
It turns into a river, like the crimson tears I used to cry
Oh, look, I'm drowning, swept away in a river of blood and ashes
And I don't care, there's nothing left, it went with the flames.
When did I . . . ? Was I . . . ?

Burning, falling, drowning. A sinner can't do much else but
Sit in a spiral of blood and ashes while fire burns all around
Can you see me? No, of course you can't, in my world of shadows
I'll go on until reticence takes me, like that will ever happen
This is the reprobation of my own sane mind,
Before it loses control again
You've told the answer but what is the question?
There is a break in the spiral, no
Just the flames devouring my mind, evaporating the last bit of guilt
I have like a dream in a nightmare
A place without blood and ashes
It's a reality that is the biggest lie
Blood and ashes, that's all there is.

Jodey Lee-Anne Sanders (14)
Ilfracombe College

Springtime

Spring is blowing in the air
Spring is coming everywhere
Spring is rising from the ground
Bringing happiness all around

The sun is shining
The birds are chiming
And the flowers are full of life

The skies are stunning
The children running
And the men are with their wives

The pretty hills
Have daffodils
With the days all getting long

But I love spring
Because of things
Like people singing songs

Spring has come
So don't look glum
And give the time some love

For making spring
A lovely thing
I thank the Lord above.

Callum Dovell (11)
Ilfracombe College

A Poem For A Friend

She laughs and she smiles, even if it starts to rain.
She'll help anyone out, if they're hurt or in pain.
She'd help me out if I was feeling down,
If seen feeling upset, she'd try not to frown.

So George is the best,
She's smiley and fun,
But she can tend to get angry
If her make-up starts to run!

And her dog Pippa,
Whom I have yet to meet,
But I hear is hyper,
And looks really sweet.

So that's my friend George,
From head to toe,
Blonde hair, blue eyes,
And a cute button nose.

Joanna Robb (12)
Ilfracombe College

True Love

Everybody deserves the chance of finding true love,
But some people never find it,
And some find it when it's too late.

But for the lucky ones,
Love is only around the corner
And they are the luckiest people in the world
Because love is the strongest emotion in people's hearts today.

Abbie Payne (11)
Ilfracombe College

Eternal Lovers

He sits all alone, with only the icy cold for company.
A cloak of darkness and fire surrounds him, but still his heart is cold.
It beats for only one thing, the one he's waiting for,
The ghostly moon, his eternal lover.
He waits for it to burst forth in victory over the sun.
When will it come?
The animal inside grows restless, but still they must wait,
Wait for the moon's silvery fire to burn in their heart.
They sit all alone, with only the icy cold for company.
Waiting for their eternal lover,
When will it come?

Bethany Parsons (13)
Ilfracombe College

My Special Friend

My special friend passed away last week,
When I realised he was gone, my heart sprung a leak.
He was great,
He was my family's best mate.
Now he is gone,
I will always mourn.
Wherever you are,
Even if you're at the bar,
I will never forget you Mick.

Jessica Floyd (12)
Ilfracombe College

My Aunty, Dying But Living A Life

I had an aunty, her name was Denise,
It broke my heart when she got her disease.
I found out she had the Big C,
It was like a thousand hot daggers in me.

She was a loving mum, wife and aunty,
All I could say is please don't leave.
The doctor told her she was going to die,
I would have rather he told her a lie,
But still she went on being so strong,
The two weeks she had left seemed ever so long.

We booked a holiday so we could get away.
We didn't have time to make a delay.
She wanted to make the most of her time,
All I wanted was her to be mine.
On the plane she was cheerful and happy,
She was changing my cousin's nappy.
We were off to Majorca for two weeks in the sun,
The rest of her life we were going to make fun.

Weaker and weaker on the holiday she grew,
Imagine if this happened to you.
A great holiday we all enjoyed,
But my aunty was almost destroyed.
On the plane all she did was sleep,
I think she may have been counting the sheep.

Straight to hospital, not a moment to waste,
I never wanted to see her encased.
My mum wouldn't let me see her,
Uncle Troy wanted to be with her,
She was too weak even to speak on the phone.

My aunty died the next day,
She painfully passed away.
I was not allowed to watch the cremation,
Hopefully she's gone to a better destination.

Jordan Hawkins (13)
Marland School

Life

Life,
Try and you will fail,
Try and try until . . .

People are going to see you how they want to see you,
People will rate you,
People will hate you,
People will love you.
We are all the same.

If you feel it and you mean it just do it,
They only put you down if you give them permission.

Everyone knows we're strange,
Everyone knows we're different,
So why do you feel ashamed?

We love you all the same,
We love you all the same,
Don't you ever change.

You're under mentioned,
Underprivileged,
Underrated and
Unappreciated

The world is turning away from us.
Just think, you have come so far after all the spitting and pushing
You have come so far after all the spitting and pushing.

Because we are all different,
Never change!

Gabby Thom (12)
Paignton Community College

These I Have Loved!

I love the smell of fresh-cut grass,
The smell of newborn babies,
The smell of disinfectant,
When the house has just been cleaned.

I love to taste of sour sweets,
Coated in grains of sugar,
The taste of hot and spicy foods,
Like the taste of pepperamis.

I love the sound of pouring rain,
As it patters on the roof,
The sound of a snake,
As it hisses in the tank.

I love the feel of fluffy cushions,
When they touch me when it's cold,
The feel when I have snuggled down,
Into my cosy warm bed.

I love the sight of pets,
When they greet you when they haven't seen you,
The sight of television,
When my favourite programme is on.

Victoria Garland (13)
Paignton Community College

Rock Pool

The teeming life of a rock pool seems oblivious to
Human life but beneath the calm, curling waves
There lies a world beyond imagination,
The hardy creatures thrive in these cool waters
Surrounded by cracks and crevasses
In the golden-brown rock.

Sean Scott (12)
Paignton Community College

My Animal House

I have a monkey,
She's always climbing around,
She's giggly and funny,
She's smelly and hairy,
I call her *oo oo argh* sister!

I have a kangaroo,
She's always cleaning up,
She bounces from here to there,
She annoyingly makes me do my homework,
I call her Springy Mum!

I have a mole,
He's always tired and grumpy,
He likes going to the pub with his mates,
He's protective over me,
I call him Sleepy Dad!

Tom Baker (11)
Paignton Community College

Poems Are . . .

Poems are boats sailing messages around.
Poems are chalk spreading words on the ground.
Poems are fish swimming with grace.
Poems are feet running at a pace.
Poems are people saying hello.
Poems are loud men that like to bellow.
Poems are water, calm and soft.
Poems are favourite things that stay in the loft.
Poems are firemen strong and brave.
Poems are bears that live in the caves.
Poems are shoes that like to dance.
Poems are the deer that like to prance.
. . . Poems are wonderful things.

Charlotte Watson (11)
Paignton Community College

My School

Today is another school day,
How I jump up and down in joy,
I don't want the day to end or I wait another day,
At the end of the day my joy is not now joy.

I am in Year 7,
And not in Year 8 or in Year 9.
As Year 7 to me is heaven,
I never want to go to Years 8 or 9.

My favourite subject is English,
My second favourite subject is maths,
My head is called Miss English.
After maths I go home and take some baths.

When the school day ends,
I never want to leave,
Because I have to wait for the next day,
I now must go home and grieve.

Connor Wooldridge (11)
Paignton Community College

Snakes

I love the sound that you make,
When you hiss at me you act like a typical snake,
Sometimes you're mean, sometimes you're nice
With your beady black eyes,
You check out all the guys,
But to me you will always be,
My lovely loyal wife.

Lauren Dawkins (12)
Paignton Community College

Things I Have Loved

Flakes of snow, falling peacefully
Dark, chilly evenings with a hot cup of tea
Sparkling Christmas lights, dazzling bright
Wrapped up in a fluffy duvet with the gas fire on

Bright beams of sun, burning immensely
Summer days at the beautiful beach
Relaxing, refreshing tropical juices
To cool you down in the summer heat

Magical coloured leaves blowing in the wind
Preparing for the winter's freeze
Running through mountains of leaves
Splashing in cooling puddle

Old oak trees blossom to green
Baby lambs cover the fields
As daffodils paint the grass
And the plants become colourful.

Nadine Fullalove (12)
Paignton Community College

Jellyfish

Body stinger,
Leg tingler,
Sea floater,
Beach founder,
Plankton eater,
Beauty finder,
Tentacle waver,
Deep diver.

Elle Keen (12)
Paignton Community College

These Are Some Of The Things I Love!

The new smell of fresh carpets
And the smell of a lovely roast dinner,
Stringy, mind-blowing cheese on a pizza,
The smell oozing out,
Shoes newly made,
The touch of springy foam
On the tip of my fingers
And the loveliness all at home,
Twizzlers revealing their taste buds,
Also the thought of being drenched, wet,
Being warm inside
And being next to a cosy fire,
With a hot chocolate in my wealthy hand,
A wardrobe full of nice clean clothes
And hating the selfishness of the rich,
As the poor don't have a clean clothes wardrobe,
The revealing, attractive chips,
The salt and vinegar hypnotising you there,
Having the family around at Christmas time,
These are some of the things I love!

Steph Sparkes (12)
Paignton Community College

If Words Could . . .

If words could dance they would dance on the ceiling
If words could sing they would sing out their meaning
If words could talk they would tell us more
If words could walk they would walk on the floor
If words were people they would be busy all day
And at night they would be thinking about what to say!

Ashleigh Vaughan (12)
Paignton Community College

Lion

Africa
Savannah plains
Crouching low in the withered grass
A golden-brown camouflage
Fixing its eyes on the unknowing prey
Prowling along the cracked, dry mud
Keeping low
Creeping slowly
Watching, waiting, listening
Hyenas laughing hysterically in the distance
Crickets and grasshoppers buzzing all around
Ears twitching with anticipation
Hind legs straighten
Moving up through the air
Pouncing, landing on top of the feast
Blood is shed
The lion is satisfied.

Holly McMahon (12)
Paignton Community College

The Otter!

In the riverbank, amongst reed beds
A nose breaking through the surface
Sleek and streamlined with silky fur
Webbed feet and tiny claws
Bobbing, turning, tumbling he plays
With gentle arrows of ripples following behind
Diving deep, sourcing shellfish
Breaking them on rocks and stones
At the end of the day
Disappearance into the bank once more.

Alice Farmer (12)
Paignton Community College

These I Have Loved

The mouth-watering smell of freshly baked bread
The stunning sight of waves hitting the rocks
Ice cream so cold and sweet on a summer's day
Beautiful rainbows, which bring sunshine after rain
Feeling safe in my duvet on a stormy winter's night

The touch of my cat's soft, silky fur
Flowers' scents filling the air
Friendly faces every day
Rain pitter-pattering on the windowpane
Home-made food, a treat for my taste buds

The familiar tone of a friend's voice
Father's hugs, which make me feel safe
A beaming moon looking down at the world
Lollies to lick when the weather's so hot
Stars which twinkle high in the sky

Smiles which light up a room
Hot apple pies so good to eat
Laughter, joy to my ears
The aroma of a familiar place
Unwrapping presents, I'm so excited

The cover of a book I'm about to read
Flowers blowing in the wind
The touch of my sister's hand in mine
The beautiful wildlife in the forests
All these things I have loved.

Sophie Glasson (12)
Paignton Community College

My Cat Suki!

You were the best cat that God lent to me.
When I got you I wish I'd thrown away the key.
But God took you back out of the palm of my hand,
I couldn't have you back in my happy little land.
You had to go, that I did know,
But wish you were still here down below.
You are now up high in the sky
And the hardest part was saying goodbye.
To my baby girl, who sleeps with me no more,
But is in my heart for evermore.
You meant the world to me
And still do little Suki.
Tears fall down my face,
I miss you baby, come and light up my living case.
You're the cat everyone wanted,
By all your memories I will always be haunted.
Maybe we will meet again some day,
Now I can't wait to see your pretty face,
Hear your loving purr and silent miaow.
Don't forget the good times Su,
I will always miss and love you!

Kirsty Jordain (12)
Paignton Community College

Dolphin

Diving, dancing, prancing,
Brushing through the waves,
Swerving, swirling, swimming,
Jumping beside the caves.
Shockingly and masterly showing off,
Its beautiful shade of grey,
With a pointed nose and a tail that shows,
Just how it grows away.

Kieran Timbrell (13)
Paignton Community College

These I Have Loved

I love the way the cool breeze blows in the morning
The way you play at night with the bright purple sky behind you
The sound of birds chirping to show that it's a new day
The taste of the hot, soothing hotpot running down my throat
The way my hamster pulls herself up and down without a care
in the world
The way my cat catches a mouse for me
The soft sleek fur running through my fingers
I love the way my mum wakes me up
I love the way the sea dances without a mistake
The way it turns white before it swallows the sand whole
And then the pebbles roll silently away.

Cheyenne Cudlipp (12)
Paignton Community College

Chameleon

Eyes of steel.
Each eye looking in a different direction.
Pupils leering on its prey.
Alternates his colour to look like bark.
He stealthily moves towards his dinner.
Still staring hard at it.
His prey is suspicious, its eyelids rapidly start to flicker.
His back legs rubbing anxiously now
As he is only two feet away.
He finally lunges at the cricket,
Snapping it up with his muscular tongue,
Then retires to the humid jungle

St John Peters (12)
Paignton Community College

Poverty

No rain, no clean water.
Nothing to wash your son or daughter.
No nice clothes or a house,
This sort of lifestyle isn't even fit for a mouse.
No doctors, no hospitals.
Everyone shouting,drop it all.
When someone sees a gun
They all stop and run.
How is this a child's way of living,
People should be giving and giving.
No hope, only despair
And people act like they don't even care.
So far away it could be like Mars,
This poor place,
A world so different to ours.

Chelsea Ewart (12)
St James' School, Exeter

A Soldier's View

Me, a soldier in a deadly war
Fighting against families and friends
People dying all around me
Guns shot, bullets flying
Bombs dropped, falling down
My friend beside me struggling
He falls, I hold him in my arms
His face so pale and sad
One last cry before the death
So please
Stop this, please.

Jodie Steer (12)
St James' School, Exeter

Love

Sad and angry because she was my friend
I still have memories of her
At Christmas, her birthday and Easter
But still I have her charm bracelet
That I gave her for a keepsake.

That's how much I trusted her
And loved her . . .
All I remember of her
Was when we had fun and went on holiday
Whatever happened?

We stood by each other because that's how much we loved
Whatever people said about us
We would comfort each other
And keep each other safe.

Now she is gone
And all I have is a lucky charm.

Rhys Anderson (14)
St James' School, Exeter

War Or Peace

When lives are lost in a senseless war
Killing innocent young people
Won't do anything to make it good
Children and women
All you are doing is condemning
And the dear departed souls will not rest in peace
Until all wars have been ceased
All the hatred and killing must end
To stop the violence that we were in
If we are to live in peace again
And if you die in this senseless war
You just made your family so angry and so sad.

Nikko Rhey Almazora (14)
St James' School, Exeter

World Peace

World peace
wars ceased
no bombs, no guns
under the sun

Smiles all around
poppies on the ground
no fighting, no dying
no people crying

No attacks from the sea
no soldiers waiting for their destiny
no rulers, no slaves
no more grenades

Rings of people
round a church steeple
no swords, no knives
no taking lives

No more wars ever
only love forever and ever
no soldiers, no wars
no bodies on floors.

Peter Hudd (13)
St James' School, Exeter

Remembrance

Rain, midnight rain,
But wild rain on this bleak hill and solitude
And me remembering again that I shall die.
Gone, gone again, May, June, July
And August but not remembered.
I'm still alive but today it is from afar that we look at life,
Death is near us and perhaps nearer still is happiness
But unfortunately not for all of us.

Abbie Hutchings (14)
St James' School, Exeter

World Poverty

I sit at home wondering,
Wondering about the homeless,
The poor, the hungry, the helpless!

I sit at home thinking,
Thinking about the children,
The adults, the babies, the helpless!

I sit at home talking,
Talking about the clothes,
The money, the homes, the helpless!

I sit at home reading,
Reading about the sickness,
The aid, the infections, the helpless!

I sit at home looking,
Looking at the sad,
The hungry, the infected, the helpless!

I sit at home listening,
Listening to the heartbroken,
The worried, the distressed, the helpless!

I sit at home wondering,
Wondering what I can do to help the helpless!

Bethan Ashelford (12)
St James' School, Exeter

How Would You Like It If It Happened To You?

How would you like it if it happened to you?
Bruises all over and severe scalds too,
Burnt with a cigarette, slept in a bath,
She never got a chance to have fun and a laugh.

How would you like it if it happened to you?
Leaving your country to start a life brand new,
From Africa to France and England she moved,
But along the way she got brutally abused.

How would you like it if it happened to you?
No one listening as you told all you knew,
But knowing if you told you'd be hurt even more,
Nobody cared that they were breaking the law.

How would you like it if it happened to you?
Your only family not caring what you do,
They needed no excuse, they just beat her hard,
She never got so much as a birthday card.

How would you like it if it happened to you?
Hospitals trying to stop her lips from going blue,
But the task they were attempting was too hard to achieve,
She died in the night but she still believes.

How would you like it if it happened to you?

Jade Ashelford (14)
St James' School, Exeter

Peace

Peace is a word
So meaningful.
Peace doesn't
Shout or scream.
Peace just sits
In the background.
Peace is about
Love and not hate.
Peace is something
That I don't see!
Peace is a world
That is different from ours!
Peace doesn't
Grow on trees.
Peace in a world
Would mean no disease.
Peace in a world
Would mean no wars.
Peace is something
That I should see!

Luke Woodman (12)
St James' School, Exeter

Peace

Love in the world, peace is quiet
Nice peace is loving and caring
Sharing is peace
Peace is like a flag waving
Never flying away and never stopping
Peace is motions of love
Peace is a beautiful flying dove
Sending love and care through the air
Peace is a sense of love just like a hummingbird
That's what peace is.

Jazmin Lovell (12)
St James' School, Exeter

World Peace

We need peace and love as big as the Earth.
In the soft wind the poppies blow around,
Listening so quietly, I can't hear a sound.
Dreams of doves floating in my head,
'Stay calm and quiet,' the little voice said.
We need peace and love as big as the Earth,
Children and couples holding hands,
Walking on the silent beach through the dusty sands.
Everybody's joking, laughing everywhere,
Troops and soldiers all declare,
The war is over now, there is nothing out there.
We need peace and love as big as the Earth.
A few teardrops in my eyes
As they say those strong few words.
Everybody cries.
No gunshots, no killing, just happiness in the air,
Just soldiers stood hand in hand,
Giving a soft glare.
We have a whole new world, a whole new birth,
We have peace and love as big as the Earth!

Abby Thomas (12)
St James' School, Exeter

What Is Peace?

P eace is love and doves
E veryone is wealthy and healthy
A live, everyone is dreaming
C an't stop people being happy
E veryone loving each other
All this and more if we had no war!

Hannah Kennedy (12)
St James' School, Exeter

Peace

Peace in the world
Everyone's silent
Poppies are covering the ground
Whilst everyone's standing round
Crying
Smiling
No one's dying
No worries but good memories
Peace is happening all around
Swords and guns have gone forever
But the evil still linger on
Pictures and belongings are all that is left
As well as gravestones with long-lasting flowers
Memorable words or phrases
Are placed where the people lay
Those are never forgotten
And are kept in their hearts all day, every day
Silence is golden
Smiling, smiling, everyone's smiling
Finally peace has arisen.

Simone Marillier (12)
St James' School, Exeter

Poverty

The sorrow,
The struggle,
In the Third World countries,
People fighting for the gift of life.

They want green,
Money and trees,
Many won't see
Clean water in their life.

No gas,
No electric,
Walk miles to wells,
Just to find them empty and dry.

Starvation,
Typhoid
And cholera,
The forms that death takes.

America's rich,
Africa's poor,
There's enough for everyone
To have a bit of green trees and money.

Terry Ryan (12)
St James' School, Exeter

Peace On Earth

People in Africa
have no food,
they have no light
but moonlight.
Sleeping in corners
with goatskin blanket
covering light.
They wake up with the sound
of their hens in the street.

Their feet as hard as bricks.
They walk for miles on end.
They have no proper shelter.
They're ill and weak without clean water.
Their animals sick with diseases that spread.

No medicines for treatment.
No transport, just walking.
No cornfields, just bread and rice.

No clothes for heat
and to stop the gnats biting the skin
but if we helped they would be thankful
for food and shelter and peace.

Nathan Beaumont (13)
St James' School, Exeter

The Lonely Kid

My family have died
and all I have left
is my pet dog
that I got via theft

My home is a mattress
and my toilet is a box
the only thing good
is my bike with no locks

I'm so sad
that I have no friends
I can't go to school
and it's the same on weekends

I cry all the time
and I sleep all the time
I've had no family
since the age of nine

My life is hopeless
I might as well be dead
because there's no point in living
so I should just chop off my head.

Nathan Langley-Bunce (12)
St James' School, Exeter

World Peace

Peace and love
make the world
go round and round,
but without them
it doesn't.

Peace and love
make people happy and joyful,
but without them
they aren't.

Peace and love
make food taste *yum!*
But without them
it doesn't. *Yuck!*

Peace and love
are good for the world
and the universe.
Peace and love is the best stuff.

Alex Hamilton (12)
St James' School, Exeter

Death

Every few seconds a person dies
The world is full of lies
Countless bullets are used
So many get confused
The bombs are on their way
Everyone's in dismay
The tanks fire, I'm no liar
Let there be world peace
Let the wars cease.

Luke Batchelor (12)
St James' School, Exeter

World Peace

No pistol, no gun,
No rifle run.
No battle, no war,
It's against the law.
No defence, no attack,
No cocaine, no crack.
No death, no loss,
No double cross.
No destruction, no explosion,
No overload.
No bust, no bang,
No shotgun gang.
No fire, no blaze,
No destruction craze.
No hunger, no thirst,
War is the worst.
No ship, no tank,
This low rank.
That's like it should,
World peace is good.

Ben Burton (12)
St James' School, Exeter

Three Things I Love About Peace

I love the way it makes us happy,
I love the way it makes us cheer,
I love the way we want it so much
And it just happens to be world peace.

Siobhan Kirby (12)
St James' School, Exeter

World Peace

I am but nine
I am but dead
I got shot by a man with a gun
He was big
I was small
He wore green
I wore white
I heard a bang
I looked down
My dress turned red
I went blue
I fell down
People ran
I cried
People screamed
I died
Tears were shed
On the mud
My family knelt round my body
They were sad to see me go.

Kayleigh Hourd (13)
St James' School, Exeter

Poverty

When I walk about in the street
I see little children with no money
Nothing to eat
Never had a mum or dad
No wonder they're looking so sad
I wonder what I can do to help them
They don't know what to do
I wish everybody could see
What's happening about poverty?

Daniel Felgueiras (11)
St James' School, Exeter

World Poverty

Poverty is a sad thing
With all these poor dying children
And children at the age of seven
Losing their parents because of AIDS.
Think if we lost our parents at the age of seven,
It would be more than dreadful because
We're not used to losing our parents at such a young age.
Imagine having to find your own food
And having no idea how to cook.
Imagine having a bad day and nobody to talk to.
Nobody to protect you and scared in the cruel world.
No one to hold you while you dream,
But you have no happy dreams anymore.
So put your hands together and say thank you to the Lord
For we are not alone nor only bone.
We are not poor or alone,
So enjoy your life because some people can't.

Shawni Wannell (11)
St James' School, Exeter

World Peace

W hat would the world be like if there was peace?
O ld and young all getting along
R ace and colour, all joined as one
L iving together, under the sun
D rought and poverty all gone

P eople stopping fighting and getting along
E nough for everyone, enough for all
A rmies of soldiers fighting no more
C easing to fight in any more wars
E veryone happy, everyone equal.

This would be world peace.

Daniel Winsor (12)
St James' School, Exeter

World Poverty

As I watch my neighbour water his lawns,
I watch on the telly as a mother mourns.
She mourns for her son, who has no water and food,
This really puts me in a strange mood,
She could have gone to Tesco's and queued.

'They don't need money 'cause they don't have shops,' says Dad,
I look at him strangely, thinking he's mad.
I touch my money in my pocket and I'm only eleven.
I hope the mum's son will go to Heaven.

The thought of people having no food or money,
Is very serious and not funny.
I ask my dad what we can do,
He shakes his head and says, 'I don't have a clue.'

I tell him the world is very sad,
He tells me, 'Yes, and quite mad.'
He tells me charity starts at home, well sort of
But I say, 'Dad we have food and water.'

I watch the telly, telling my dad, the world does not make sense,
He tells me it never will because
The people who can change things just sit on the fence.

Ashley Hudd (11)
St James' School, Exeter

Our World

If you sit and think today
About your life in every way,
You will see that in our time
Some people's lives are unrefined.

They walk for miles to get a drink
And when they see it their hearts must sink
For it's infested, full of dirt
To carry it home must really hurt.

They have diseases,
They're so unwell,
They can't keep clean,
They probably smell.

People have no homes in many places
The whole world over, there's many cases,
They live on the streets the whole year through
In winter's frost they're out there too!

So sit and think of how you live
And also think of how to give.
The smallest offer or token given
Can bring a smile and make a life worth living!

Daniel Bond (11)
St James' School, Exeter

Hope

At last . . .
No more fighting
No more hurt
No more bombs on the Earth.

No more noise
No more people dying on the Earth

No more people frightened, people in a house,
No more bombs touching the Earth.

At last . . .

People happy
People love

People loving the whole wide world.

Rebecca Hannah Ellis (12)
St James' School, Exeter

Victoria

She was from the Ivory Coast
The place she loved the most
She moved to London
Only to be unloved
She was made to sleep in a tub
And a cheap plastic bag
She hated London
She was abused
She was lucky to have shoes
She had fag burns on her back
The police didn't do anything
. . . Until the time she was laid in a box.

Tom Marshall (14)
St James' School, Exeter

Say No To War!

No more crying
No more dying
No more sadness
But lots more happiness

No more arms being blown off
No more legs being blown off
No more bombs being dropped
This has to stop

No more nightmares
No more dark stairs
No more frights
But a few more scary nights!

Sarah Wakeley (12)
St James' School, Exeter

Victoria

From Ivory Coast
To London centre,
Starved, living on toast.
She slept in a sack
And was stabbed in the back.
Scolded on the head,
Without a bed.
Until one day,
She was out, astray.
She was killed, dead
And she stayed forever in a wooden bed.

Dan Chadwick (14)
St James' School, Exeter

No Hope

Children crying
Children dying

No rain
Too much sun

Flies crawling on bodies
Not just children, everybody

Can't read
Can't write

No clean water
In sight

Nothing to play
Every single day

They're so skinny
They need money

Don't let their bones rot away
People die every day

Just give them money to help them say:
'This tastes nice' or even, the best thing of all, *smile*

Make poverty history
Please give money to help their lives!

Bradley Riley (11)
St James' School, Exeter

We Want World Peace!

When two armies line up to fight
When bombs are dropped from a height

We want world peace
We want war to cease

Towns destroyed in a click
Just like a stone getting flicked

We want world peace
We want war to cease

Cities destroyed as easy as towns
The winners come over in leaps and bounds

We want world peace
We want war to cease

Happily thieves destroyed and killed
Which takes years to rebuild

We want world peace
We want war to cease

People happy to kill themselves to win
Just as easy as putting out the bin

We want world peace
We want war to cease.

Holly Montague (12)
St James' School, Exeter

No More War

No more war,
It should be against the law.
No more bombs,
Sing happy songs.
No more deafening weapons,
Stop the family separations.
No more palaver,
Bring back my father.
No more loved ones dying,
Seriously, I'm not lying.
No more people that fear,
Stop the eerie atmosphere.
No more racism,
Their experiences are humanism.
No more errors are made,
Rules have to be obeyed.
No more go their way,
Can't wait to come home in May.
No more danger,
Things have to change.

Estelle Hacq (12)
St James' School, Exeter

War!

Sadness, death and killing galore,
This happens in war that we want no more.
Buildings collapse and people die,
Little children always cry.
Tanks blown up and arms blown off,
When the dirt comes up the people cough.
The women are screaming, the men are dying,
The teenagers running and babies crying.
Children die and people are sad,
The people killing are the people that are bad.

We want peace in our lives,
Clean up the world so we don't kill with knives.
No more killing and no more dying,
So children can play with no more crying.
Families can live in harmony and peace,
Children don't scream and parents don't panic
And people don't run around go manic.
So no more war, no more lives lost,
People don't fight at death's cost.

Jamie White (12)
St James' School, Exeter

A Poem About World Peace

Peace is all we want
In this world right now
All the fighting and poverty
We need to stop it now

The world is a beautiful place
That we live in here and now
Treat it with respect
And see how it grows

The evils of the world
Are what we have made
So spread a little happiness
Express your views out loud

In our souls we have peace
In our hearts we share
Let's all join together
And show how much we care

What we want in this world
Is peace and harmony
No famine or poverty
Just love and peace.

Charlie Otton (11)
St James' School, Exeter

Poem

This world lives in harmony
And people suffer in different countries
Because of lack of childcare.
Some are good and some are bad,
But they all abuse children
In different ways.
Cigarette burns and beatings
And many more,
Take Victoria, some beaten friend,
She was beaten and made to starve -
Though she is dead she is not forgotten.
Bandages and plasters all over,
This is the work of the bad
And the good prevent it from happening.
Be safe and keep on hour guard
Because the bad is all around,
It is like one mined battlefield
And you're battling for your life and soul
But know a barrier has protected you -
The social worker has come to.

Declan Croft (11)
St James' School, Exeter

Africa

Living in Africa
Where children stay,
In the nasty world
Where they can't play.

Living in Africa
Where there is no food,
They are drinking from a river
All day long.

Living in Africa
Where they sleep,
Sleeping on a road
All their lives.

Living in Africa
With no one,
All alone,
Very scared.

Living in Africa
Where children don't have anyone,
Starving to death.

Living in Africa
They are starving,
Never had anyone
To help them get food.

Living in Africa
Where their families are lost
Don't know where they are going.

Bethany Gunn (11)
St James' School, Exeter

Living In Poverty

No one for me -
No breakfast or tea,
I'm living in poverty.
So much neglecting
And little protecting,
I'm living in poverty.
There is no love
And little care,
The world we live in is not fair,
I'm living in poverty.
Hope is a beauteous thing
But it has disappeared,
The danger of the harsh, cruel world has happened
Just as I feared,
I'm living in poverty.
So many diseases
So easy to get,
So hard for people to just not fret,
I'm living in poverty.
What's happened to the world
With all its wondrous glory?
It's sold itself out to money and greed
And for poor countries in need, there's no happy story,
I'm living in poverty.
Just think right now,
About the catastrophes in all the different places,
Who's going to take the blame for all the sad and confused faces?

Eve Murchison (11)
St James' School, Exeter

Africa

Across the African plains
Where animals roam free
People hunt for trophies
With guns and flee
The people poor
Walk miles for water
Bake bread on the floor
And cook on a platter
The sun always shines
All hot and bright
They have landmines
Now that's not right
Children play and have fun
Play all and run
Mums and dads work hard
Just to stay alive
Like bees in a hive
There are big cats and small
Elephants and things that crawl
It's a colourful place.

Emma Teague (11)
St James' School, Exeter

World Poverty

World poverty is a bad thing,
What does it bring?
Why does it sing?
Our mums and dads do anything.

How could I breathe
When I can't heave?
But my health couldn't stay,
Nobody could be wealthy.

I am so down
And I always frown,
I really need more than a pound.

World poverty is horrible,
Nobody can be bothered,
Nobody can hover,
They need to be undercover.

Can they stay together
For ever and ever?
Nobody wants to help them, never,
They don't want to stop them.

Danielle Whitehead (12)
St James' School, Exeter

World Poverty

Why can't there be no world poverty
in Africa and India and more?
Why can't everyone have enough money to live?
Why can't there be enough food to eat?
Why, why, why?

All over the world, people are suffering
because they have no food to eat or water to drink.
Children are dying because they have no food for their bellies.

Wives hoping their husbands can find work
to feed and clothe the family.
Children feeling sad, bored and lonely
because they have no toys or friends to play with.

Put an end to world poverty, get rid of all the corrupt governments.
Give the people in Africa tools and seeds
to grow their own food.
Stop the madness, save the children.
Give the children a childhood.
Help them! Help them!

Ben Hough (11)
St James' School, Exeter

What Is Money?

What is money?
Does it give us happiness
Or do we feel we have less?
People argue over it,
Starve over it,
But when do we stop?
Is it really worth something?
I'll let you be the judge of that!

Vanessa Murphy (14)
Stoodley Knowle School

Only See

The night brings different people, ideas, stories,
People cower behind closed doors and curtains,
Not knowing what goes on whilst they sleep.
Babies lie in their cots, dreaming.
Not knowing what goes on past their mobiles of colourful rainbows and teddies.
You can use as many metaphors as you like.
Cover it with stars and planets, owls and wolves.
Romanticise the moon and the sun,
But as soon as the sun sets, the people come out in their hordes and gangs.
Who knows what lies under their jackets.
Knives, guns or perhaps some car keys and a stick of gum,
But their shifty eyes suggest something else.
You can't help but think you're better than them just because you're in your car.
You wind up the window, push down the car lock,
But what if you stopped?
Just for a second. Maybe if you asked, they might tell you great works of Shakespeare,
Sing to you Mozart's concertos
And then, then you'd know not to judge by the stern eyes,
The non-existent smile, the unshaven face.
The outside.
Then it wouldn't matter to you that it was dark, for it would seem as bright as day.
It wouldn't matter about the greasy hair and scuffed up shoes,
Because all you'd see is an angel.
If you only had eyes and no brain, you would not be able to judge.
Only see.
If you could only see, then you would see a person and not a group.
Changing what is really there.
Only see.
Not changing, discriminating.
Only see.

Hannah Snow (14)
Stoodley Knowle School

My Lips Are Sealed

I can't stop thinking about your smile,
about your eyes, I melt inside.

I may be just a no one,
I don't matter at all,
but when you talk to me,
I feel special all the more.

I wish I didn't love you,
all it brings is pain.
Every day I am knowing,
you will never feel the same.

I am just a girl to you,
but to me you're my world.
I would do just about anything
just to be curled . . .

Up in your arms,
never let me go,
hold me tighter,
but you see you'll never know,

So I'll keep it my secret,
I will be forever bottled up inside,
next time you talk to me,
I will have to hide . . .

My feelings for you, they're so strong
I'm bursting to shout out,
I will love you forever,
it will never run out.

But I still can't tell you,
even if I wanted to,
because you don't feel the same.
If you said no
I would run out of your life,
just dying in shame.

I tell you all my secrets,
I share with you my world,
but there's one thing I haven't told you,
I can't,
I won't,
my lips are sealed.

Bonnie-Belle Summer Showers (14)
Stoodley Knowle School

Dreams

When night falls I go to sleep,
My thoughts dance in my head.
Some thoughts are happy, some are sad,
It's my world I visit in my bed.

Dreams are something special,
They are messages from the heart.
Dreams are what hold people together,
Nightmares tear people apart.

Dreams let me escape my life,
They let me wonder and explore.
In my dream I'm someone different,
I'm taller and stronger and sometimes more mature.

When I wake my dreams are over,
Whether I was in space or by the sea.
In the morning I think them through,
And I realise my dreams reflect on me.

Rebecca Barton (14)
Stoodley Knowle School

Friendship

Friendship is like the breeze,
You cannot taste it,
Smell it,
Hold it,
Or know when it is coming.
You can always feel it though
And you will always know it's there.
It may come then go,
But you know it'll always be back.
You may not always like someone
And they might not like you,
But the important thing about friendship is,
It's always open to you.

Lauren Boitoult (14)
Stoodley Knowle School

Untitled

Isolation and loneliness,
Desperation with no happiness.
With wings outstretched,
She waits in the darkness.

The silhouette disappears,
As she lays drowning in her fears.
The cold evaporates around her,
She waits in the darkness.

Her heart longs for something,
Something to take the pain and anguish away.
All she can do is let the tears fall,
Fall as she waits in the darkness.

Georgia Ruskin (14)
Stoodley Knowle School

The Soldier

He lay in peace all on his own,
His family had no clue at all.
He was a kind young gentleman,
Who was unlucky and didn't get away in time.

As the soldier lay there on the ground,
Nothing was heard, there was no sound.
The gun was sitting by his side,
That he had in his hand as he died.

The soldier had felt feelings of happiness in his life
And problems of trouble and strife.
All thoughts of evil had gone inside,
As he lay in the corner of a foreign field.

Katie Loader (14)
Stoodley Knowle School

Untitled

I saw the sea glittering.
It reminded me of you.
Even the waves lapping gently,
Reminded me of you.
I still love you Nan, even though you're gone.
When I look at your photo, you make me smile.
I think of your voice, always telling a joke,
Then I stop. What's the point?
You're not here,
You left me . . .
All alone.

Elena Visser (14)
Stoodley Knowle School

A Light In The Distance

What is that light
Coming nearer and nearer?
Is it her?

It is still coming closer,
Nearer and nearer,
But still not a stir.

Why is she coming
After years of searching?
Could it be?

Yes, she is closer,
Now in full vision.
Yes, it is she!

She holds out her hands,
Coming nearer and nearer,
Not saying a word.

I just can't believe this,
How could it be her?
This is absurd!

She holds my two hands,
Her fingers like ice,
Speaking my name.

'My darling, I love you,'
She said in my ear.
I feel the same.

She's fading away now,
Further and further,
Saying goodbye.

Further and further,
Melting away,
Oh why, why did you die?

Lois Noon (14)
Stoodley Knowle School

Just Listen

Just listen.
We always talk,
But just listen.

Listen to a friend who might be in need,
Listen to the voices which are full of greed.
If we never listen, we will never know,
If we never listen, we will never grow.

Just listen.
We always talk,
But just listen.

Listen to the people who are lonely inside,
Listen to the people who just try to hide.
They might be full of anger and think nobody cares,
But if you just listen, they'll know you are there.

Just listen.
We always talk,
But just listen.

We might think that everybody else is the same,
'They don't care about me, I'm just another name.'
But maybe some people do care, and aren't just pretend,
Maybe some people will always be our friend.

Just listen.
We always talk,
But just listen.

Abigail Ellyatt (14)
Stoodley Knowle School

Untitled

Jimmy was going to school today,
It was his first day in big school,
He entered the gates, went through the big doors,
He just couldn't find his way!
He asked a girl for some help, but she shoved him out of the way.
'Ring a ding ding'
The bell went for lunch,
Jimmy walked into the hall,
No one would sit next to him,
So he sat on the floor, alone.
The big boys came over and pushed him about
And finally, they stole his lunch.
Jimmy was sad for the rest of the day
And went and sat on the toilet.
Soon after, he was followed by some older kids
Who shoved his head down the loo.
Jimmy didn't come into school the next day,
Nor the next day after that.
Teacher would say, 'Hmm, where's Jimmy?'
Pupils would snigger and laugh.
They found Jimmy a few days later,
Lying on his bedroom floor,
Empty tablet bottle in hand.
'Oh no!' they all screamed,
No one was laughing then.

Anna-Marie Milstead (14)
Stoodley Knowle School

Life As We Know It

Why are we here today,
In this world of ours?
The more we do,
The more we do to our world.
If we had the chance to change our lives,
We'd accept it.

Change our world, don't destroy it,
World pollution is because of us.
Run the world on less power,
Don't intoxicate the oceans and rivers.
Use less electricity to help our world.

If we change our world now we will live on,
Through generations,
We got here because of others.
Don't waste it.

Ashley West (11)
Teignmouth Community College

Away With Words

I sit on the bench as I cry and cry,
I have just been told that I'm going to die.
I am distraught and my family are too,
My eyesight is blurry and I am feeling quite blue.

I have just three months to live,
But I don't ever want to die,
I'm making the most of the time I've got left.

Ashleigh Tibbs (11)
Teignmouth Community College

Away With Words

Bombs dropping, guns firing,
People suffering, people dying.

Gassing rooms, exhaust pipe fumes,
Travelling up the pipe,
In through the windows,
Nothing to live for, attempting suicide.

No food, no shelter,
No clothes, no money,
No Dad, no Mummy.
They're both gone now,
War is to blame for it.

They whipped him, they hit him,
They kicked him, they slashed him,
Then for the last one,
They strung him up by his neck,
No life, the end of his life.

Lee Price (11)
Teignmouth Community College

Away With Words

I am distraught, tears well up in my eyes
I suddenly find out this has all been lies
The never-ending whiteness, no reason to live

My child is gone and so is my wife
No reason to take my last stride
No family, no person to take my fall
I think I might leave now for a very long time.

Oak McMahon (11)
Teignmouth Community College

Away In A Dreamland

Away in a dreamland,
far away.
Someone searches
for a day.
That's lost inside
their mind of dreams,
out of reach
forever it seems.
Their eyes are full of sorrow,
their hope is shattered and bent,
inside their heart is broken
on dreams they can't fore tend.

Emily Pearce (11)
Teignmouth Community College

Away With Words

Why are we here?
Will I ever know?
One day we come, another day we'll go.

Do I have a purpose?
If so, what could it be?
Are we really meant to be?

What is the point?
Don't you see?
We don't matter, you and me.

Lydia Vincent (11)
Teignmouth Community College

Me And Time

I'm just a kid,
so what can I say?
I'm bored to death,
so what can I do?

In my parents' day,
they'd play with the simplest thing,
not! the hi-tech games of today.

But if I could turn back time
and live this life again,
I'd live like my parents.

I'd follow their every moment,
to get the discipline I deserve,
Gulp! I don't want the belt.

Oliver J Newton-Browne (11)
Teignmouth Community College

Away With Words

T owers
W obble and
I ntercept
N ow

T umbling
O ver and over
W ill
E ventually
R each the helpless people on the
S treets!

Luke Mathias (12)
Teignmouth Community College

Time

Time is a river
that never stops flowing.
It is wind that never stops blowing.
It's everywhere,
it's invisible.
Time is slow,
when things are dull.
It is fast when things are fun.
Eat a bun pretty fast,
enjoy it while it lasts.

Katy Robinson (11)
Teignmouth Community College

The Winter's Litany

I see the snow cover the trees,
That's God's gift.
Children chucking cold snowballs,
That's God's gift.
Families inside their cosy homes,
That's God's gift.
Giving presents by the tree,
That's God's gift.
Dogs digging in the snow,
That's God's gift.
Fluffy white clouds above our heads,
That's God's gift.
Watching snow turn into men,
That's God's gift.
The sun comes out to dry the snow,
That's God's gift.

Jamie Barker (11)
The King's School

Babies!

Babies can cry,
Babies can laugh,
They splash around in the bath.

Some can be happy,
Some can be sad,
Some drive you crazy,
Some make you mad!

Most babies are quite fun,
They make you hide,
They make you run.

They make you read stories,
They make you read books,
They think it's funny when you give them strange looks.

Some are boys,
Some are girls,
Some have straight hair,
Some have curls.

Most of all babies are there,
For you to love
And to care!

Kelly Birchmore (11)
The King's School

My Dog Jonty

Jonty, my favourite pet
Never wants to go to the vet
On the way to getting old
The dog that's always bold
You know he'll be there.

Ollie Weeks (11)
The King's School

Out Of Bounds

A boy stared out of his window,
He longed to explore the grounds, but they were out of bounds.
At the stroke of midnight, way past his bedtime,
He crept down the creaking stairs, the door creaked open.
He stepped out into the night,
The wet mist caught his legs like snares.
He tiptoed down to the ice house,
He knew about the catacombs that stretched far beneath,
He rattled on the door, to his dismay the rusty padlock was
still in play,
He picked up a rock off the ground, hit the padlock once.
From inside came a sound.
Something old and frightening pulled itself to the keyhole.
It blinked, it could not contain itself with glee, one more hit!
Crack! The padlock broke, the boy wrenched open the door.
The being within and the boy outside saw each other's
gleaming eyes.
The boy screamed but the dry hands pulled him in . . . !
There was a reason it was out of bounds.

Harry Bird (11)
The King's School

Horses

I'm small, I'm tall,
I'm wide, I'm fat; hey, don't call me that,
I can walk, trot, canter, run,
Saddle me up, we'll have good fun.

I have big feet and I'm nice to meet,
I spend all my time in a field all day,
My favourite food is fresh hay.

But when I go for a ride with my friend,
I hope this day will never end,
But oh it does!

Carla W-B (11)
The King's School

Out Of Bounds

Climb over the wall
grass and moss is everywhere
and it is silent

The windows are smashed
the walls are old and crumbling
cobwebs all around

It is really dark
the door is hanging open . .
why not go inside?

Rosie Lane (13)
The King's School

Jail

My life is off limits,
My family is out of bounds,
My home is forbidden,
But that's too hard to understand.

Why can't I be trusted
To live the life I made?
Things I've loved and lived for
Haven't taken long to fade.

The grass outside, that jagged fence,
Sways happily with glee,
But it's jeering, mocking, taunting,
Wild and wistfully free.

As I sit inside my jail cell,
I'll offer this advice:
Don't let good things become out of bounds -
Don't waste away your life.

Elspeth Darkin (12)
The King's School

Out Of Bounds

I am not used to this area,
It is not my home.
My country has left me,
To fight a war.

I am a refugee,
In another country.
All my rights and help,
Have vanished into eternity.

To some people,
From this and other countries,
They might say that
I am out of bounds!

Sam Brandom (13)
The King's School

Summer

I love the tall apple tree fluttering lightly in the warm breeze
Gently waving its outstretched arm
With its neat shiny green leaves
Dancing joyfully at its fingertips

I love to see the stripy buzzing bees gliding
Gracefully between the snow-white daisies
Collecting powder-like pollen with their tiny feet

I love the twittering birdsong
Echoing through the trees
As they sway to the tuneful song of summer

I love the dazzling ray of yellow sun
Reaching out across the clear blue sky
Like an outstretched arm
Shimmering as the world goes by.

Natasha Harmer (12)
The King's School

Out Of Bounds

Who's to say what I can and can't do?
I don't believe I'm any different from you.
But still you bind me with your chains of safety,
You say it's for my own good,
But it's *your* fears that contain me.
You know I can't walk and I know that too,
But why would that stop me from living life to the full?
Too many times I've been left behind
Never to reach the finishing line.
I long for a place where people see *me!*
Untie my binds and let me fly free,
So I can find that life is not out of bounds for me.

Charlotte Hipperson (13)
The King's School

A Normal Day!

A normal day
A normal walk
The normal way
The normal talk

Then it appears
In front of my eyes
And as I near
The moonlight dies

The darkness glooms
Around this place
I feel like I'm
In outer space

I have to go
Not meant to be here
The light is back
And the mist has cleared.

Laura Dickinson (11)
The King's School

Summer

Silky touch of butterfly wings
Brush past the apple trees
Filled with harmonious choir birds
Singing melodies just for me

Green grass filled with daisies
Waves to a cloudless clear blue sky
Watching idly as a bird or two
Flap their great wings by

Swans glide elegantly
On a crystal fairy lake
Snowy head held proudly
Eyes glinting, wide awake

Flowers in their satin dresses
Green arms held aloft in a ballerina stance
Swaying to the sound
Of a distant bubbling brook
Dancing their entrancing summer dance
While the green trees onward look.

Alice Lynch (11)
The King's School

Is There Something Out There?

Is there something out there?
Lurking in the night,
Sitting on the lamp post, giving me a fright,
I went out to see,
Nothing was there,
Since then I've been wondering,
Was it really there?

Tom Hodgson (12)
The King's School

Out Of Bounds

'Tis silent all apart from the sign,
It swung, squeaked and read *No Entry,*
I had been here many times before,
Never been in, never since the day,
The day which pricked every hair on my back,
The day which made ghastly winds settle
And roaring tempests turn into calm seas,
No one spoke of the day,
Too frightened that it would happen again I suppose,
As for many of them the screams still rang
Through their heads like a fire drill,
I still could hear the pitter-patter of the feet running for their lives,
I could hear the evil high-pitched cackle of the 'madman',
This would haunt me till my dying days,
I was only a child when I was huddled in the corner
Watching like a mouse in a house full of cats,
As the place burnt, exploded and smouldered,
The day when the door was locked and never opened.

Natalie McKay (12)
The King's School

Flower

One solitary flower standing brave
More to follow in a couple of days
Soon a big bunch with trumpets up high
The colour of honey from a beehive

One solitary flower standing brave
More to follow in a couple of days
Soon a big bunch with petals out proud
Spectacular flowers right down to the ground

All this from two solitary flowers.

Emily Light (12)
The King's School

Out Of Bounds

I'm trapped, beaten, deserted,
I'm swollen, lost, defeated.
I'm kicked out of my house by fear.
It's out of bounds; I'm startled!

The house is like a raging fire,
Exploding, popping, it is dire.
All the screaming, shouting is crackling and roaring.
It's out of bounds; I'm frightened!

I'm trapped, deserted, beaten,
I'm swollen, lost, defeated.
Locked out of school by dread,
I'm trapped, I'm abandoned!

The school is like a prison,
Locked away, forbidden.
Locked out of school by apprehension.
I'm trapped, I'm dumped!

Luke Rutter (12)
The King's School

Out Of Bounds

A lone building standing small in the corner,
Fences all around standing guard, waiting for nothing,
Still silence covering up everything,
Lonely stacks of bricks standing ready to be built upon, if ever,
Hard hats waiting on the floor, waiting for nothing,
Tools lying amongst rubble, waiting to be used, although they never will,
Everything is waiting for nothing, but nothing ever comes.

Grace Pulteney (12)
The King's School

Poverty

Poverty isn't a crime, a punishment, a disease,
It's nothing,
As it stares us back in the face.

People are helping, just not enough,
Because it's still there, still alive,
Staring us back in the face.

Stuck in mounds full of sand, full of nothing,
No water for miles,
Just staring us back in the face.

No smiling, no laughter, no happiness,
Blank faces with no life worth living,
Staring back into our face.

Rice is all they live on,
Nothing else is there, nothing else exists,
Staring us in the face.

A lump full of emptiness,
A life full of destruction,
Staring us in the face.

Poverty isn't a crime, a punishment, a disease,
It's nothing,
Staring us right in the face.

Robyn Caldwell (11)
The King's School

When I Grow Up

When I grow up, what will I be?
Fighting fires or out at sea?
Will I be off to war, discovering islands, or studying law?
Will I police the land, join the circus or sing in a band?

When I grow up what will I be?
Roller skating or climbing a tree?
Will I be scaling up on a cliff, working late or doing shifts?
Will I be making or baking pies, deep sea diving or flying the skies?

When I grow up what will I be?
Will I be scoring for England or making tea
Will I be writing for books and mags, making shoes or selling bags?
Will I be designing clothes so fine, building a house or learning
my lines?

When I grow up what will I be?
Will I be famous, rich and sure?
Will have children to love and adore?
Will I be happy, content with all that is mine?
Will I find worthwhile ways to fill my time?
When I grow up what will I be?
One thing's for sure . . . I'll always be me!

Tom Bowern (11)
The King's School

Out Of Bounds

Stop! No further!
Don't come here.
You're not welcome,
We don't want you.

You can't sing,
You can't dance,
You have no talent,
Nothing.

'Please, let me in!'
No, you are nothing,
You can't come in.
Leave us alone.

Strictly not allowed,
No useless wimps,
We are the best,
So, go away!

Ellie Veasey
The King's School

Out Of Bounds

I walked along the dark corridor,
Downstairs I hear her voice tinkling like bells,
The lights on the stairs turn off,
The air gets stuck in my lungs.

A floorboard creaks as I open the door,
The room inside is dark.
The only light is the moonlight pouring through the window,
No one must know I am here.

Alicia Gibson (13)
The King's School

Siren's Note

The world goes hazy with a whisper of a note in the air,
My insides turn watery, my head numb.
I have a flashback of the happy parts of life,
Being born, starting school, making my first friends,
Starting secondary school and then finally leaving school
and getting married.
Then it all dissolves into a big dark whirlpool,
My feelings spin around and around making my head burn,
I fall to the ground crying out loud,
I'm alone, hearing only this note in the air.
The note possesses me, leaving me blank and empty,
I hear the words coming closer to my heart, closer, closer, *closer!*
I close my eyes, my heart pounding inside,
The song pulls me apart leaving me with a vision of my last
few moments.
'Death is here' the song says to my brain, I feel a thump then I go
flying up into the air,
In love with this note I fall victim to death.
Without my soul inside my body, my brain sings the note of death
over and over again.

Ben Jennings (13)
The King's School

Out Of Bounds

Alarms. Sirens. Flashing lights.
Guards running. Guards shouting.
The barking of a dog.
Grey gates shutting smoothly.
Shiny silver sections of razor wire.
Reflecting the light of the floodlights.
A fugitive. Crouching in the shadows.
As quiet as a mouse.

Sam Scott-Perry (13)
The King's School

Out Of Bounds

He slithers like a snake
He's as swift as the wind
He growls like a tiger
His feet make no sound
He sneaks around cities
He strikes in the dark
He waits for a victim
His gun at the ready
He attacks like a lion
He runs like a gazelle
He disappears into the darkness
Like he was never there.

Katherine Perrington (12)
The King's School

Out Of Bounds

I could see it now,
I edged closer, closer.
through the door,
I tiptoed, tiptoed.

My mother's voice,
It echoed, echoed.
You've had quite enough,
Quite enough, quite enough.

Through the door now,
I crept, further, further.
Towards the tin,
Slowly, slowly . . .*yes!*

Mmm in my mouth,
It melted, melted.
The sweet taste of . . .
Chocolate, chocolate!

Hannah Bird (12)
The King's School

My Best Friend

Eyes green and yellow,
Like a dream when fast asleep.
Her beauty soft as a lullaby,
Or many a tear to weep.
Hair of burning copper,
Skin as pale as peach,
Many a time her hand
I would need to reach.

Heart of gold,
But not as strong as you might expect.
A friendship we have,
I will never forget.
My best friend Sally,
A gem I would say,
Her spirit as bright as a clear sunray.

Isheeta Abdullah (13)
Trinity School

Autumn Days

Going for long walks
Crunching through the leaves
Thinking as I'm walking
Smelling the dewy breeze

Curling up on the sofa
With a cup of tea
Thinking about the summer
And fun memories

It's only 6 o'clock
And already it's dark as midnight
Watching the hours pass by
There needs to be more light.

Rhiannon Depla (13)
Trinity School

Autumn Days

Depressing! That's all it is
The dead vegetation laughing at you
The leaves turn dull
And they twist and turn around you

You walk along the path, to different places
As you see all the familiar faces
With the dying sun splashing all around them
As they run to their hidden dens

The wind rushes all around my head
I really want to just curl up in bed
The sounds of the rain, patter on the roof
Everyone acts so aloof

The dark shadows of the woods
As its different colours change the mood
The dead flowers lie at your feet
As you look at the leaves that's like a blanket sheet

The clouds cover the sky
Their foreboding colours say goodbye
The trees, so dark
As the dogs start to bark.

Mia Hayward (13)
Trinity School

Autumn Fun

The roaring fire, crunching through its fuel, log by log.
Lighting up the cosy room in which we gather.

The burning embers draw people in from their daily routine.

Summer is a thing of the past.

As the leaves slowly wither and fall to the dew-tipped
blades of grass frosted with ice.

Piles of golden leaves crunch as young feet
proudly patter through them.

Excited voices are fascinated with the games
in which autumn has created.

The orchards are busy as their fruits develop.

Pumpkins alight with their frightful expressions.
Telling a story for children to hide.

As darkness draws closer, still early it would seem.
Back to the fire, awaiting its gleam.

Melissa Downey (13)
Trinity School

Deadly

Deadlier than T-rex
But with teeth nowhere near as large.
Deadlier than a lion,
But not as large a bite.

Deadlier than a raptor,
But with claws nowhere to be seen.
Deadlier than a polar bear,
But with much less muscle.

Deadlier than a cheetah,
But lots are fat and slow
And deadlier than a turtle,
But a shell is not seen.

Deadly to its own kind,
Deadly to its own self,
And deadlier than anything bigger or smaller,
More powerful, quicker or harder.

The deadliest thing that has ever lived;
Humans, mankind,
People.

Jonathan Hadley (14)
Trinity School

The Autumn Months

Autumn, summer's over, leaves falling,
Brisk walks down country lanes,
Lambs growing, farmers getting ready for the harvest.

Autumn, summer's over,
The vision of cold dark nights, roasting marshmallows,
The jolly songs round the fire,
The wholesome moon watching over us.

Autumn, summer's over, nearly Christmas!

Harry Locke (13)
Trinity School

An English Autumn

Chestnuts roast on an open fire,
The dew rests on the morning grass,
Darkness comes swiftly, like a dashing wolf,
Crackling leaves; an orange vixen,
Fruit drops from trees, succulent and plentiful,
Charming spaniels, no longer cubs,
Harvest arrives while winter threatens,
Crystal rain, showers from Heaven,
Sun piercing, breaks the gloom,
Poppies rise and tulips wilt,
Toughened fish struggle against the stream,
Woodland creatures drink from brooks,
Blackberries ripen, delicately sweet,
Summer's gone but autumn's here,
Enjoy it, winter beckons,
Hallowe'en ends this vivid season,
Apple bobbing and pumpkin heads.

Jamie Isaac-Richards (13)
Trinity School

The Leafless Trees

The leafless trees sway in the brisk wind.
The brown, yellow leaves gently flutter down to earth.
The conker trees filled with juicy ripe conkers.
Crunching, crackling leaves on the lanes.
Farmers moving sheep from field to field.
Dew on the crisp green grass.
Bees searching for the last pollen.
People playing rugby in the last summer sun.
Children play outside for the last time.

Tristan Wiggins (14)
Trinity School

The Wilting Autumn Rose

The weather starts to change,
The dew lies all around the rose,
It is alive.
The petals start to darken,
Getting colder, colder,
It is dying.
The world around it is quiet,
All of the leaves, trees and grasses are gone,
There is nothing.
The last of the colour is drained from the petals remaining,
Everything is dull and dark.
The last petal of the rose's life falls to the ground,
The rose is dead.
Never to live again.

Danielle Jones (14)
Trinity School

Winter's Coming

Fires glowing, chestnuts roasting,
Hilltops glistening, leaves crunching,
Darkness coming, summer leaving,
Lambs growing, frost is falling.

Fruit ripening, conkers falling,
Rugby's starting, cricket's finished,
Harvest collecting, robins whistling,
Bees buzzing, hats on.
Winter's coming.

Will Plunkett (13)
Trinity School

Autumn Leaves

Willowy winds rustle in the trees,
Lifting leaves, whistling through the air,
Oranges, red and mellow yellows,
Flying all around.

Flying past windows,
Where the young embers glisten and glow,
On the charcoal-scorched wood,
Then moving on past, to somewhere anew.

Racing past the murky river,
Flowing over rooftops with smoke pouring out,
Plummeting to the ground,
Until they are next stirred.

Ellis-Jayne Taylor (13)
Trinity School

Autumn Time

I step out onto the dew,
Covering the lawn like tiny beads of glass,
A wave of frigid air,
Bites at my skin with a cold nip,
The darkening clouds,
Bring down a haze of drizzle,
Dampening the world,
The leaves emblazoned with the colours of fire,
Floating softly, softly to the ground.

Emma Roby (13)
Trinity School

A Chorister's Autumn

Walking, shivering, running, shouting, whispering, walking,
Walking through a dark, smug, misty cathedral green at evening,
Remembering that back at school, a bed and warm food awaits,
All twenty, tranquil after singing evensong, crunching leaves.
Whispering boys in suppressed joy of warmth,
How one laughs as you slip on a wet, brown, slimy, crunchy
appealing leaf.
A shout and all goes wild, laughing, joking, shouting,
Hang up your mortar board, gown and run.
A stampede, a crowd at the food table,
Chicken!
Hot chocolate!
After five minutes nothing but clattering cutlery and banging mugs
are heard.
All run back to the boarding house.
A hug from matron and then a shower and bed,
Warm under the duvet, snug.
All quiet and dew creeps over the ground outside.
Morning comes soon.
Oh, how a chorister's autumn is so magical.

Matthew Smith (13)
Trinity School

My Autumn

The golden red leaves providing the perfect backdrop
to this season of my life.
Back in school, the corridors ringing with the busy sounds
of creative minds, waiting to be engaged.
The weather, dark and gloomy, rain bringing on colds and Calpol,
but then the leaves fall, the trees are laid bare.
Winter is here.

Sam Homer (13)
Trinity School

Young Writers Information

We hope you have enjoyed reading this book - and that you will continue to enjoy it in the coming years.

If you like reading and writing poetry drop us a line, or give us a call, and we'll send you a free information pack.

Alternatively if you would like to order further copies of this book or any of our other titles, then please give us a call or log onto our website at www.youngwriters.co.uk

Young Writers Information
Remus House
Coltsfoot Drive
Peterborough
PE2 9JX

(01733) 890066